Sexuality

A GRAPHIC GUIDE

MEG-JOHN BARKER & JULES SCHEELE

ICON

Published in the UK and the USA in 2021 by
Icon Books Ltd, Omnibus Business Centre,
39–41 North Road, London N7 9DP
email: info@iconbooks.com
www.iconbooks.com

Sold in the UK, Europe and Asia by
Faber & Faber Ltd, Bloomsbury House,
74–77 Great Russell Street,
London WC1B 3DA or their agents

Distributed in the UK, Europe and Asia by
Grantham Book Services
Trent Road, Grantham NG31 7XQ

Distributed in Australia and New Zealand by
Allen & Unwin Pty Ltd,
PO Box 8500, 83 Alexander Street,
Crows Nest, NSW 2065

Distributed in Canada by
Publishers Group Canada,
76 Stafford Street, Unit 300
Toronto, Ontario M6J 2S1

Distributed in India by
Penguin Books India,
7th Floor, Infinity Tower – C, DLF Cyber City,
Gurgaon 122002, Haryana

Distributed in South Africa by
Jonathan Ball, Office B4, The District,
41 Sir Lowry Road, Woodstock 7925

Distributed in the USA by
Publishers Group West,
1700 Fourth Street,
Berkeley, CA 94710

ISBN: 978-178578-653-2

Originating editor: Kiera Jamison

We mention a number of authors and books throughout this introduction. Bear in mind that **speech bubbles attributed to these authors should not be read as direct quotes** – they're often paraphrased to give a sense of that author's ideas.

Printed and bound by Clays Ltd, Elcograf S.P.A.

SEXUALITY: GOING TO THE PLACES THAT SCARE US

Sex is sold to us – and used to sell all kinds of things – with the promise of great pleasure, liberation, and self-understanding. It's also a topic fraught with confusion, contradiction, and danger. Although sex is everywhere around us in wider culture, it's something that most of us actually know very little about because of:

- Stigma around talking openly about sex – even with people we have sex with
- Fears around educating kids about sexuality
- The very limited understandings of sex and sexuality that make it into mainstream media, therapy, or sex advice.

Get BEACH BODY READY NO...

BE HARDER AND LAST LONGER WITH THIS NEW

Time's up on sexual harrassment.

what's up?

I sent him naked pics and now everyone has seen them. I'm scared to go to school.

ARE YOU A SEX ADDICT?

HOMOPHOBIC HATE CRIME ON THE RISE

CULTURAL ANTHROPOLOGIST GAYLE RUBIN

OUR CULTURE DRAWS AN EVER-SHIFTING LINE BETWEEN SEXUAL ORDER AND CHAOS. IF ANYTHING IS PERMITTED TO CROSS THE LINE, WE FEAR THAT THE BARRIER AGAINST SCARY SEX WILL CRUMBLE AND SOMETHING UNSPEAKABLE WILL SKITTER ACROSS.

SEXUAL FEAR AND SHAME

Despite sex being everywhere, it remains taboo. Most of us hold a great deal of anxiety, embarrassment, and shame about our erotic desires and attractions, our bodies and our desirability, and the ways we do – or don't – engage in sex.

Our sexuality is often seen as an essential aspect of our identity – revealing truths about us that have implications far beyond what we do sexually. We fear discovering that we're sexually abnormal or dysfunctional and that this might mean there is something more fundamentally wrong or bad about us.

Fear, shame, and confusion around sexuality are understandable. People are still killed, imprisoned, cast out of their families and communities, medically or psychologically treated, and stigmatized, bullied and discriminated against for having the "wrong" kind of sexual desires, having sex with the "wrong" types of people, or at the "wrong" times. There are huge potential costs to acting on our desires, and to not acting on them. And sex is often bound up with our yearnings for love and belonging , and fears of pain and rejection.

PLEASURES AND POTENTIALS

Our sexuality may also be our passport to pleasure, joy, success, and/or liberation.

- Sex can be one of the most exciting, pleasurable, even transcendent, experiences that many people have
- Being sexually attractive and desirable to others often brings power and success
- Sex provides the possibility of deep, intimate connection with another human being: of being utterly seen and wanted for who we are
- Sexual attraction can be a key component in the excitement of "falling in love" and bonding with partners
- Our sexual desires may reveal much about our inner lives

- Sexual freedom can be linked to personal and political liberation
- Through our sexual – or asexual – identities and shared experiences we may find community and belonging with likeminded people
- Claiming our sexualities – or asexualities – and being open about them can feel a vital way of being authentic, real, and proud.

MULTIPLE MEANINGS OF SEXUALITY

Sexuality refers to both: the constellation of **social** meanings that our wider culture attaches to sex and our deeply personal **individual** experience of the erotic.

Sexuality is **socially constructed**: our society develops and passes on strong messages about what is sexual, which sexual behaviours are acceptable or not, and what it means to have a certain sexuality, through media, laws, education, medicine, and science. At the same time, we all have a **lived experience** of sexuality which involves our bodies, feelings, and desires, and which shapes our relationships and wider lives. Sexuality is both within us and in the world. How we see our and others' sexuality informs which erotic experiences are available to us. People have different experiences and can resist dominant messages about sexuality, and this is part of how cultural understandings shift over time.

Sexuality includes, but is about more than, just having sex. It also includes: our capacity for sexual feelings; the kinds of people we're attracted to and how; and how we identify ourselves and how others categorize us.

INTERSECTING SEXUALITY

Sexuality can't be separated from other social structures and our position within them. The way sexuality operates – and how we experience it – is intrinsically bound up with: gender, race, class, disability, nationality, ethnicity, age, generation, geographical location, faith, and more.*

KIMBERLÉ CRENSHAW

* Much gratitude to Kimberlé Crenshaw and all the other intersectional feminists and critical race theorists who have pointed this out over the years.

OUR SEXUALITY JOURNEY

If we're going to fully understand sexuality, we're going to need to confront our social and individual ghosts, monsters, and demons. This book aims to be a friendly guide through this potentially scary, uncertain territory.

CHAPTER 1: THE INVENTION OF SEX

It may sound strange, but the ways we currently identify our sexualities, understand our desires, and have sexual relationships all came into being pretty recently. We also remain haunted by the ways of understanding sex that have emerged over the centuries.

HISTORICAL HAUNTINGS

Sexuality is also haunted by the ghosts of all those who have been hurt or lost their lives because of the ways sex has been understood, and policed, over time:

Women who died in childbirth, who had no reproductive rights or access to birth control; people sterilized, killed, and denied relationship rights during eugenic attempts to keep nations "pure"; black slaves who were repeatedly raped by their "owners" because they were regarded as property; sexually diverse people – and understandings – wiped out during colonization; and those who died from HIV/AIDS and other STIs due to lack of available contraception and prevailing attitudes towards sex.

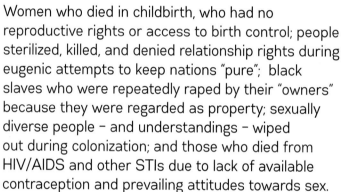

We see the legacy of these historical traumas in the stereotypes – and treatment – of disabled people, people of colour, working-class people, sex workers, women and queers, in relation to sex.

A POTTED HISTORY OF SEX

In this chapter, we'll explore how we've arrived at our view of sexuality in the West – and how that view has been imposed on others around the world. We'll visit ghosts who draw our attention to the dangers of limited understandings of sex, and we'll explore the social structures and forces that informed – and enforced – these views.

We often assume that the way sexuality is understood and expressed in the time and place we currently occupy is right, normal, and natural. Looking across time – and around the world – helps us to see that things have been different, and could be different again.

Looking back helps us to understand why our current understandings of sexuality feel so entrenched. They carry the heavy weight of history. Changing them would require huge individual and social shifts, as well as acknowledging the serious damage that we have caused by reproducing them and passing them on.

BEFORE SEXUALITY: THE CLASSICAL WORLD

CITIZENSHIP FOR FREE ATHENIAN MEN WAS A SEXUAL AND GENDERED CONCEPT AS WELL AS A POLITICAL AND SOCIAL ONE.

CULTURAL THEORIST DAVID HALPERIN

Historians have called Ancient Greece and Rome a period "before sexuality" because sex had such radically different meanings then. The erotic was part of public life, intrinsically linked with social and political order.

Men in Ancient Greece demonstrated their dominance over others by penetrating them, including all women, male slaves, foreigners, or younger aristocratic boys. Enjoyment of the "passive" role of being penetrated was culturally stigmatized, associated with femininity and submission.

Male desire for both men and women was so taken for granted that there were debates over which was the superior form. It was suggested that armies should be composed of male lovers since warriors would be brave to impress each other.

Due to the everyday struggle for survival, there was more cultural anxiety around food than sex, although over-indulging in either was seen as a problem, and self-control was highly valued. Women were viewed as lacking such self-control and had the status of minors, although there were some examples of recognition of women's desire for each other. Such women were regarded as inappropriately masculine.

13

CHRISTIANITY

Early Christianity shifted away from the Greco-Roman ideal of having self-control, and away from the Jewish celebration of fertility, which included desire within marriage.

THE BODY IS A TEMPLE TO THE HOLY SPIRIT AND MUST REMAIN PURE.

PAUL THE APOSTLE

The Christian ideal was to have no desire and to avoid all sex unless for procreation. Lust was linked to humanity's expulsion from Eden. Jesus asked that his disciples be unmarried. Celibacy and purity were revered. Gradually these ideas filtered into popular consciousness and began to be supported by laws forbidding adultery, divorce, and "sodomy".

HAD GOD CONSULTED ME IN THE MATTER, I WOULD HAVE ADVISED HIM TO CONTINUE THE GENERATION OF THE SPECIES BY FASHIONING THEM OUT OF CLAY.

MARTIN LUTHER
PROTESTANT REFORMER

However, early Christianity did open up possibilities for non-sexual erotic/ecstatic experiences and for close same-gender relationship bonds.

MEDIEVAL PERIOD

Historian Eleanor Janega points out that in the Middle Ages, "sodomy" referred to any kind of sex that couldn't result in procreation.

All extramarital sex was regarded as sinful, and marital sex should be untainted by desire given that desire endangers the soul. Married couples were encouraged to have **penis-in-vagina (PIV) sex** quickly.

> AVOID KISSES AND TOUCHES AS THEY PROCEED FROM LUST AND ARE MORTALLY SINFUL.

PHILOSOPHER AND PRIEST THOMAS AQUINAS

> SOD THAT!

There were rules restricting sex to certain days of the year, times of day, and to clothed missionary position sex – only when the woman wasn't menstruating or nursing. Women were viewed as more sexual – and more able to enjoy sex – than men in medieval Europe. This distinguished them from men, as closer to animals.

> WOMAN'S LOVE IS EVER INSATIABLE; PUT IT OUT, IT BURSTS INTO FLAME; GIVE IT PLENTY, IT IS AGAIN IN NEED; IT ENERVATES A MAN'S MIND, AND ENGROSSES ALL THOUGHT EXCEPT FOR THE PASSION WHICH IT FEEDS.

THEOLOGIAN AND PRIEST SAINT JEROME

THE ENLIGHTENMENT

During the Reformation of 16th and 17th-century Europe, the Protestantism of Luther and others – alongside the scientific revolution – disrupted the hold of Catholicism. Secular rulers became more powerful, and concern shifted from policing inner sin to outer crime, distinguishing private and public life.

Many intellectuals proposed the pursuit of happiness as the most important goal in life, which eventually became enshrined in the United States Declaration of Independence. Many linked the pursuit of happiness explicitly to sexual pleasure, writing erotica as well as philosophy, and using pornographic works to criticize religious and political authorities. So sex became linked to freedom and liberty, and viewed as a private matter.

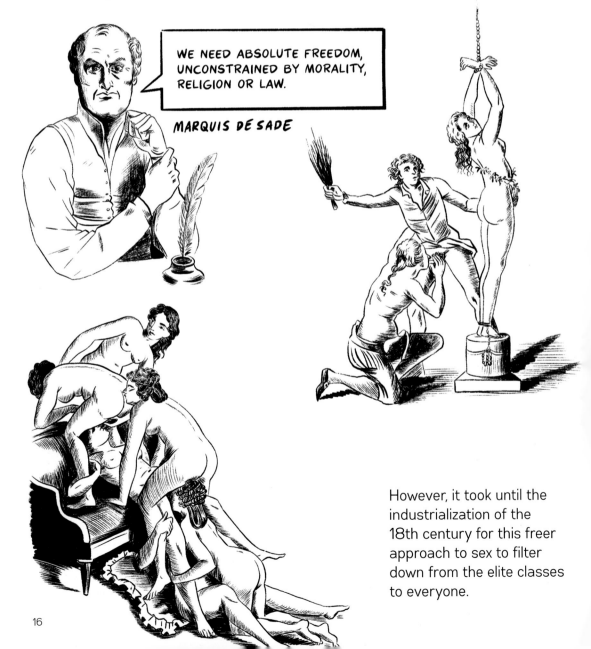

WE NEED ABSOLUTE FREEDOM, UNCONSTRAINED BY MORALITY, RELIGION OR LAW.

MARQUIS DE SADE

However, it took until the industrialization of the 18th century for this freer approach to sex to filter down from the elite classes to everyone.

SEX HIERARCHIES OVER TIME

So, across time and place good, acceptable sexuality has generally been differentiated from bad, unacceptable sexuality, but how they are differentiated has differed a lot: penetrator vs penetrated; honourable vs shameful; controlled vs excessive; chaste vs desiring; for procreation vs for pleasure; natural vs unnatural; harmful vs beneficial.

Sometimes women have been seen as less sexual than men, sometimes more so. Whichever way around, in these patriarchal societies, this has always involved women being seen as inferior and sexually questionable.

By the 18th century, the understanding of women as lecherous and seductive had been reversed and they were seen as sexually passive and at risk of seduction by men. This was probably because men's sexual behaviour was no longer so curbed by religious rules– enshrined in law – except in relation to sex with other men, which was regarded as unnatural.

> WHEN MORALISTS PRAISE AS A VIRTUE WOMEN'S WANT OF PASSION, I AM DISGUSTED. WE CANNOT ENDEAVOUR TO PLEASE A LOVER BUT IN PROPORTION AS HE PLEASES US.

> THE MAJORITY OF WOMEN (HAPPILY FOR THEM) ARE NOT VERY MUCH TROUBLED BY SEXUAL FEELINGS OF ANY KIND.

PHILOSOPHER, WRITER, & WOMEN'S RIGHTS ADVOCATE *MARY WOLLSTONECRAFT*

PHYSICIAN *WILLIAM ACTON*

THE INVENTION OF SEXUALITY: VICTORIAN PERIOD

During the 19th century there was a backlash against the perceived dangers of libertine approaches to sex, following the horrors of the French Revolution. Concerns about crime rates and the impact of population growth on food supply led to churches and governments attempting to manage desire again.

As more and more people worked outside the home, the private sphere became idealized, as did love between husbands and wives. Marriage was deemed the appropriate place for sex to happen. Romantic love, sex, and happiness became intertwined in ways that continue to this day.

The emerging capitalist model was of men going out to make money, and women working unpaid in the home, caring for and reproducing the workforce. For this reason men and women became seen as increasingly opposite: men as strong, ambitious, and not showing emotion or vulnerability; women as passive, delicate, nurturing, and dependent. This combination was romanticized, and also regarded by scientists and medics as natural sexual expression. In this way gender, sexual, and relationship normativity became linked together, enshrined in the ideal of the married, romantic male/female couple who had PIV sex with each other.

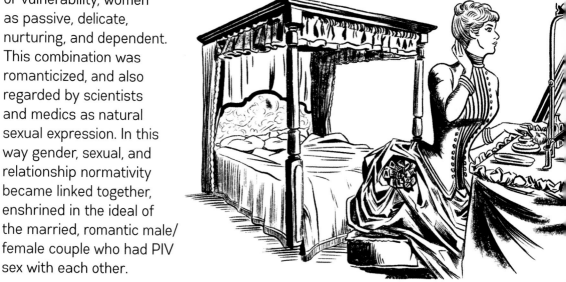

SEXOLOGY

At the turn of the 20th century sex became an object of scientific study. Influenced by Darwinian theories of sexual selection, sexologists deemed reproductive instincts natural and normal, and everything else as a form of deviance to be categorized and explained.

Sexologists classified these so-called "perversions" in weighty tomes, often only published in Latin in an attempt to keep them from the masses.

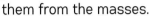

I'M GOING TO NEED TO GET A LATIN DICTIONARY...

The COPROPHILIC
The UNDINIST
The SADOMASOCHIST
The FROTTEUR

Sex became seen as a potentially overwhelming natural force and therefore a source of both individual and social disorder. Urbanization also made it more visible, with sex work and men having public sex with other men. The law was increasingly called upon to delineate normal from abnormal sex in determining whether people were criminals.

The normal/abnormal distinction became a key way of viewing sex, conflated with healthy/pathological, innocent/criminal, and good/bad binaries. Thus sex required control through medicine, law, and education.

THE CREATION OF A SPECIALIZED, DESPISED, AND PUNISHED ROLE OF HOMOSEXUAL KEEPS THE BULK OF SOCIETY PURE IN A SIMILAR WAY TO THE WAY THE TREATMENT OF SOME KINDS OF CRIMINAL KEEPS THE REST OF SOCIETY LAW-ABIDING.

SOCIOLOGIST MARY McINTOSH

THE INVENTION OF HOMOSEXUALITY AND HETEROSEXUALITY

For the first time, sexualities were scientifically and popularly regarded as identities people *had* rather than activities they *did*, associated with particular character traits.

The invention of "homosexual" as an identity resulted in the invention of "heterosexual" as an identity also. However, initially "heterosexual" was used to mean people with depraved interests in acts other than procreative sex, just with the "opposite gender". The still-present heteronormative idea of heterosexuality as the "natural" default sexuality took hold later.

> SODOMY HAD BEEN A TEMPORARY ABERRATION; THE HOMOSEXUAL WAS NOW A SPECIES.

PHILOSOPHER AND AUTHOR OF *THE HISTORY OF SEXUALITY*, MICHEL FOUCAULT

Many sexologists conflated same-gender desire with gender, but in differing ways. "Inversion" models saw homosexual men as feminized, and homosexual women as masculinized. However, other models saw homosexual men as hyper-virile, heroic and masculine.

The idea of "the homosexual" as a particular kind of person with a fixed identity formed the basis of arguments for gay rights through the 20th century. We'll return to this in the next chapter.

> THE INVENTION OF THE HETEROSEXUAL AS PART OF THE PROMOTION OF GAY RIGHTS IS ONE OF SEX HISTORY'S GRAND IRONIES.

HISTORIAN & AUTHOR OF *THE INVENTION OF HETEROSEXUALI* JONATHAN NED KATZ

CONFESSING SEX

The idea that we should *confess* our sexuality dates back to early Christianity. In defining sex as shameful, taboo, and revealing of the mind's deep desires, Catholicism paradoxically fostered an incessant reflection on sex, and the telling of sexual stories.

This Christian ethic echoed through the libertine's pornographic fiction, and the patient case studies written up in sexological texts, both of which involved the telling of hidden sexual truths. We still see this in agony aunt columns, reality TV and reality dating shows today.

One of the many contributions of the father of psychotherapy, Sigmund Freud, in the early 20th century, was to make delving into your sexuality something for everyone rather than just something for the "abnormal" subjects of sexological texts. While Catholic confession was about preventing people from sinning – or atoning for sins – the aim here was alleviating mental health problems.

I CONNECTED SEXUAL DEVELOPMENT TO ALL OUR EVERYDAY NEUROSES AND DEFENSES. THE "TALKING CURE" OF THERAPY WAS MY WAY OF ADDRESSING THESE. BY SPEAKING OUR UNCONSCIOUS DESIRES PEOPLE COULD REACH GREATER SELF-UNDERSTANDING.

THE SEXUAL REVOLUTION

Freud was influential in refocusing on pleasure as the aim of sex, rather than procreation.

Building on Freud's ideas, later thinkers, such as Freudian Marxist and author of *The Sexual Revolution*, Wilhelm Reich, linked sexual repression directly to individual neuroses and social ills.

WILHELM REICH

AUTHORITARIAN SOCIAL ORDER AND SEXUAL SUPPRESSION GO HAND IN HAND. REVOLUTIONARY MORALITY AND GRATIFICATION OF THE SEXUAL NEEDS GO TOGETHER.

FULL AND PERFECTED LOVE REQUIRES ACCESS TO THE KNOWLEDGE OF HOW TO CULTIVATE IT.

MARIE STOPES

Others, such as scientist and author of *Married Love*, Marie Stopes, produced early forms of sex advice presenting pleasurable sex as a vital part of happily married life.

During the 20th century, the contraceptive pill and women's rights movements furthered the sense of women's entitlement to sexual pleasure. The free love movement unhooked sex from marriage. This was furthered by consumer capitalism which presented

happiness as something everyone should aspire to – often selling products and lifestyles using images of sexual pleasure.

The ongoing tension between sex as a source of pleasure and of danger re-emerged in debates between moralists and liberals – and between different schools of feminists – around abortion, gay rights, sex work, and pornography, for example.

A MAN MUST WOO A WOMAN BEFORE EVERY SEPARATE ACT OF COITUS.

UNDERSTANDINGS AND EXPERIENCE

In 1936, sexologist Havelock Ellis described a married woman horrified to discover she had been masturbating for years without realizing, and now faced "moral ruin".

In Ancient Greece, this woman would've been reassured by medics like Galen and Hippocrates that regularly releasing her "seed" would prevent blockages.

From medieval times until recently, she would have faced punishment and judgement. In the 18th century, she would have been told masturbation leads to hysterical fits, violent cramps, nymphomania, and other ills.

In the early 20th century, the likes of John Harvey Kellogg (of breakfast cereal fame) would have recommended cold water, vigorous exercise, or even electric shocks to curb the habit.

In the 1970s, feminist consciousness raising groups would have encouraged her to continue masturbating to learn about her sexual pleasure. Today sex therapists advise masturbation as part of sex communication, but warn against it becoming an addiction, especially if it involves porn.

Shifting prevailing understandings of all aspects of sexuality markedly impact how we experience it.

IF I KEEP HAVING THESE BAD DESIRES, I'LL BE A MARATHON RUNNER IN NO TIME!

THIS IS OK BECAUSE IT'LL IMPROVE SEX WITH MY HUSBAND.

GLOBAL VARIATION

Looking around the world, as well as over time, demonstrates how sexuality is socially constructed.

ANTHROPOLOGY HAS SHOWN THAT WHAT IS CONSIDERED "SEXUAL" HAS VERY DIFFERENT RANGES OF MEANING ACROSS CULTURES.

CULTURAL ANTHROPOLOGIST PHILLIPS STEVENS JR
*WRITING IN THE INTERNATIONAL ENCYCLOPEDIA OF HUMAN SEXUALITY

EARLY MUSLIM SCHOLARS WERE TALKING ABOUT SEX IN A VERY STRAIGHTFORWARD WAY AS A NORMAL, POSITIVE PART OF LIFE, NOT PURELY TIED TO PROCREATION, MARRIED, OR MAN/WOMAN RELATIONSHIPS.

HISTORIAN & AUTHOR OF HOMOSEXUALITY IN ISLAM, SCOTT SIRAJ AL-HAQQ KUGLE

This means that people also experience, express, and make sense of their sexualities in very different ways. For example, around the time that Christian ideals of sexual sin were taking hold in Europe, the *Kama Sutra* and other Hindu manuscripts in India were teaching techniques to achieve sexual satisfaction and divine ecstasy as part of living well.

Most cultures over time have had rules against incest and rape, but how these were defined and punished differed widely. For example, in UK law up until 1991, marital rape was not recognized as a crime – or even a possibility.

CULTURAL DIVERSITY

Cultures differ in how they view same-gender attraction and sex across generations.

Many cultures don't separate gender and sexuality in the current Western way but rather see them as woven together, often interconnected with spirituality.

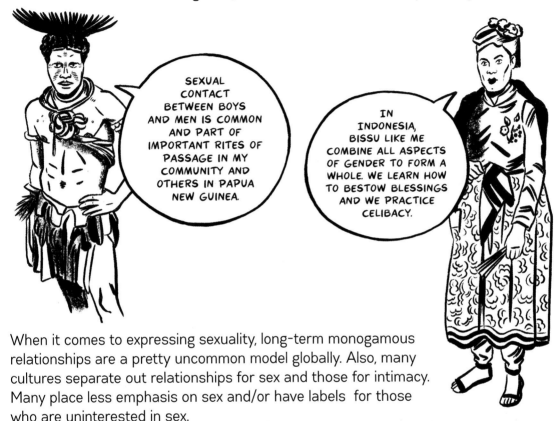

SEXUAL CONTACT BETWEEN BOYS AND MEN IS COMMON AND PART OF IMPORTANT RITES OF PASSAGE IN MY COMMUNITY AND OTHERS IN PAPUA NEW GUINEA.

IN INDONESIA, BISSU LIKE ME COMBINE ALL ASPECTS OF GENDER TO FORM A WHOLE. WE LEARN HOW TO BESTOW BLESSINGS AND WE PRACTICE CELIBACY.

When it comes to expressing sexuality, long-term monogamous relationships are a pretty uncommon model globally. Also, many cultures separate out relationships for sex and those for intimacy. Many place less emphasis on sex and/or have labels for those who are uninterested in sex.

IN JAPAN MANY SINGLE MEN IDENTIFY AS HERBIVORES. THEY'RE NOT NECESSARILY WITHOUT ROMANTIC RELATIONSHIPS, BUT ARE GENTLE AND HAVE A NON-ASSERTIVE, INDIFFERENT ATTITUDE TOWARD DESIRES OF FLESH.

AUTHOR MAKI FUKASAWA

From such cultural diversity we could draw the lesson of reflecting critically on any assumed "normal", "natural" form of sexuality, but instead we often sensationalize such variation in popular media, presenting it as an object of fascination to be explained or challenged by Western "experts".

ETHNOCENTRISM AND SEXUALITY

Psychologist and author of *Perv*, Jesse Bering points out that, while the extent of erotic diversity across time and place is breathtaking, it has often been hard to see this diversity due to the prudishness and ethnocentrism of Western anthropologists. Many ignored sex entirely until recently, or imposed homophobic and other normative understandings on the people they studied.

There have been similar problems with the study and portrayal of sexual communities *within* Western cultures. The legacy of sexology has meant that many social scientists and media producers still focus on labelling and *explaining* sexualities outside the norm. We see this in the "freak of the week" format of sex-related TV shows.

HETERONORMATIVITY IS THE REAL MONSTER

As we'll see in Chapter 4, classifications of perversions from early sexological texts to the present day read like demonologies: lists of the monstrous desires which – like demonic spirits – could inhabit us, take us over, and make us disordered or diseased.

What if the real monsters are not those categorized as sexually "abnormal" and seen as mad or bad but instead are the powerful systems and structures that have imposed such limited ideas of sex and sexuality on all of us over the years, and still do? Who is the monster really, underneath? To determine this, we need to understand how the history of sexuality is interwoven with that of gender, race, disability, and class.

We've already seen how gender, sexuality, and relationships became inextricably linked: "normal" sexuality involved attraction to someone of the "opposite" gender, expressed through certain kinds of sex (predominantly PIV) within a monogamous couple. This idea that heterosexual sex, relationships, and gender roles are superior is called **heteronormativity**.

PATRIARCHY IS THE REAL MONSTER

Heteronormativity is an example of a **patriarchal** understanding because it relies on the idea that men and women are inherently different in ways that disadvantage women. For example, we've seen how heteronormative sex (PIV) is actually not the most pleasurable kind of sex for many women. It carries a high risk of STIs and pregnancy.

Strikingly, despite the meanings of sex and sexuality changing dramatically over time, women have always been regarded – and treated – as inferior to men. Whether seen as sexually passive or active – as "madonnas" or "whores" – women's sexuality has been regarded as a problem, and their bodies and expressions have often been altered to make them more sexually desirable and/or to police their sexuality.

The modern form of the sexual double standard expects men to be naturally lustful, whereas women have to walk a fine line between being seen as a "slut" or a "prude". The impact of this can be seen in pressure on women to be sexual in order to retain relationships, in the high rates of sexual violence against women, in victim blaming when they speak out, and in stigma against sex workers (whorephobia).

COLONIALISM AND WHITE SUPREMACY ARE THE REAL MONSTERS

Prevailing understandings of sexuality are also closely linked with the enslavement and colonization of others.

One way that African slavery was justified by Christians was on the basis of their belief that black people carried the Biblical "curse of Ham": having engaged in incest.

The genocide of Two Spirit people was part of settler colonialism in the country now called the United States of America. It was justified on the basis that they didn't conform to colonizers' understandings of sexuality and gender.

Under British Imperialism, scientists divided people into normal/superior and abnormal/inferior to justify colonizing those deemed inferior. This categorization carried over into the study of sex. Legal scholar Chan Tov McNamarah points out that societies in which colonizers imposed anti-queer laws still see high levels of queerphobia in the present

day – and vice versa. White Westerners often paint other cultures as inherently less tolerant of sexual minorities, enabling them to scorn them and to deny their own complicity.

The legacy of this includes the tendency to regard some racial groups as more or less sexual than the white "norm". For example, the common sexual harassment of black women (seen as hypersexual and as property), and frequent panics around black and brown male sexual predators, even though the majority of people convicted of sexual offences are white (and race is hardly ever mentioned in such cases).

BODY NORMATIVITY IS THE REAL MONSTER

Historically, the project of categorizing people's sexualities into "normal" and "abnormal" is intrinsically linked with the ways in which certain bodies have been defined as normal and "disordered" in Western culture. This has roots in both colonialism and the eugenics movement.

Early 20th-century eugenicists discouraged mixed race relationships, as well as believing working-class and disabled people to be inferior – and less worthy of reproducing. Far from being a minority view, many prominent European and American sexologists were eugenicists, such as Havelock Ellis, Marie Stopes, and Margaret Sanger. We can see the legacy of such approaches in the way that disabled people are frequently viewed as non-sexual.

WE NEED TO PREVENT PEOPLE WITH UNDESIRABLE CHARACTERISTICS FROM REPRODUCING AND TAINTING THE POPULATION.

MARGARET SANGER

Fat activists also point out how norms have been created around body shape and size in a similar way to sexuality, gender, race, and disability. Fatter bodies are still deemed unhealthy because of the false equation of being outside the "norm" with moral inferiority and physical or mental ill-health.

The legacy of all of this remains in the dominance of white Western ideals of sexual attractiveness (young, slim, pale-skinned, straight hair, etc.).

OMG BECKY

LOOK AT HER BUTT

CAPITALISM IS THE REAL MONSTER

We've seen that industrial capitalism required women to work unpaid in the home, and to reproduce. So sexuality and sexual relationships are intrinsically connected to the economic order, class, and the financial valuing of some labour (male, upper/middle-class) more than other (female, working-class).

As with racial "Others", working-class women have often been portrayed as sexually available or insatiable, to be kept apart from middle-class women in case of adverse influence on them. The devaluation of women's labour, this separation based on class, and perceived sexual availability feed into whorephobia: prejudice against sex workers.

Sex has been interwoven with consumer capitalism from the inception of modern advertising, with the "sex sells" ads of the 1950s, to today's ads, which fuel anxieties about sex and bodies in order to sell us products to "fix" them.

SEX SELLS!

NEOLIBERAL CAPITALISM HAS BROUGHT A TURN FROM SEXUAL OBJECTIFICATION TO SEXUAL SUBJECTIFICATION. INSTEAD OF OTHERS POLICING OUR SEXUALITIES, WE POLICE THEM OURSELVES.

GENDER SCHOLAR & AUTHOR OF *MEDIATED INTIMACY*, ROSALIND GILL

INTERGENERATIONAL TRAUMA

Fantasies of what our sexualities could – and should be – are continually produced and sold to the next generation. Sexual stigma and shame could be seen as a kind of intergenerational trauma which is perpetuated when each generation fails to address it and simply passes on the problematic messages they've learnt about sex.

WE MUST REJECT ANY FRAMEWORK THAT MAINTAINS HOMOSEXUALITY AS A CATEGORY OF DEVIANCE THAT NEEDS TO BE EXPLAINED AND INSTEAD FOCUS ENTIRELY ON THE ORIGINS OF, AND SOLUTIONS TO, HOMOPHOBIA AND HOW IT IS PASSED ON THROUGH FAMILIES.

QUEER ACTIVIST & AUTHOR OF *TIES THAT BIND*, SARAH SCHULMAN

Younger generations are at the forefront of endeavouring to understand sexuality in more diverse, inclusive, intersectional ways, but they're up against great opposition.

YOU CAN'T SAY ANYTHING THESE DAYS WITHOUT BEING DONE FOR SEXUAL HARASSMENT. STRAIGHT WHITE MEN GET THE MOST PREJUDICE NOW. ALL THESE INVENTED TERMS – ALRIGHT THEN, I IDENTIFY AS A PENGUIN! DON'T LOOK OFFENDED; YOU'RE ALL SUCH SPECIAL SNOWFLAKES.

DUDE, WE SEE WHAT YOU'RE DOING.

I WOULD'VE GOTTEN AWAY WITH IT TOO, IF IT WASN'T FOR YOU PESKY KIDS.

SEX IS THE BIG STORY

Recent sexologists argue that sexuality is totally interwoven with all the current social issues we're facing. Social movements are often also sexual movements.

Sociologist Jeffrey Weeks points out that sex has been integral to all the major social and political crises of the last century, from early 20th-century eugenics and the suspicion around homosexuality during the Cold War, through the blaming of gay people for AIDS and the decline of the family in the 1980s, to the #metoo movement , #BlackLivesMatter, and the trans moral panic, including the ways in which black men and trans women are framed as potential sexual threats to justify state sanctioned violence against them.

> THE TRUTH IS THAT SEXUALITY IS EVERYWHERE: THE WAY A BUREAUCRAT FONDLES HIS RECORDS, A JUDGE ADMINISTERS JUSTICE, A BUSINESSMAN CAUSES MONEY TO CIRCULATE, THE WAY THE BOURGEOISIE FUCKS THE PROLETARIAT, AND SO ON.

…SOPHERS

…S DELEUZE &
…K GUATTARI

Debates about sexuality are debates about the nature of society, and vice versa.

> SEX HAS BECOME THE BIG STORY. PEOPLE ARE ENCOURAGED TO TELL THEIR SEXUAL STORIES IN PUBLIC, WITH DIFFERENT STORIES HAVING THEIR TIME TO BE TOLD.

SOCIOLOGIST & AUTHOR OF *TELLING SEXUAL STORIES*, KEN PLUMMER

LEARNING FROM THE GHOSTS OF THE PAST

Historical shifts have shaped the ways of understanding and experiencing sex that are available to us today.

Remember that this book itself is situated in a particular time and place. We haven't got to the "right" understanding of sexuality now. Our understandings will always be constructed and contextual. People in the future will see what we haven't seen - or can't see - now.

CHAPTER 2: SEXUAL IDENTITY

We've begun to see how sexuality became understood in the way it is today. Over the next four chapters we'll explore different elements of sexuality starting with sexual identity, or orientation.

We'll bring these threads together in Chapter 6 to look at why our own particular sexualities end up the way they do.

As we've seen, there's no one true way to understand sexuality. However, the Western world operates as if there were. One particular understanding is reproduced across medicine, therapy, law, education, and media relating to sex. With globalization, this narrow view has been increasingly imposed around the world, as well as on many people in the West who don't fit it. In the coming chapters, we'll also learn about how sexuality actually works from those who resist, refuse, or reinterpret common understandings.

WHAT IS (YOUR) SEXUALITY?

Think about how you'd respond if asked to put your sexuality on a form or dating app. The app is probably relying on the most common understanding of "sexuality" as meaning our sexual **identity** – or **orientation** – defined by the gender of the people we're sexually attracted to (who we orient towards).

Generally it's assumed that we either orient towards the "opposite gender", in which case our identity is straight, or the "same gender", in which case our identity is gay.

So, our sexuality, according to the mainstream view, is based on a combination of our gender and the gender we're attracted to. As an identity, it's also assumed that our sexuality is a fundamental and unchanging part of who we are.

In this book, we'll explore other ways of understanding sexuality and many more labels beyond "gay" and "straight".

FREUD AND POLYMORPHOUS PERVERSITY

We saw in the last chapter that early sexologists invented this sense of having a fixed heterosexual or homosexual identity.

Sigmund Freud developed these ideas and brought them into common-sense understanding. He divided sexuality into the object (who we're attracted to) and the aim (what we want to do with them).

Freud's theories have been enormously influential in creating the sense of a fixed sexual identity based on our gender and a binary gender of attraction.

THE STRAIGHT/GAY BINARY

The straight/gay model is a **heteronormative** model as well as a **binary** one. Freud saw heterosexuality as the normal outcome of sexual development and homosexuality as a deviation from it.

Freud's followers entrenched the idea of homosexuality as a pathology in the psychiatric and psychotherapeutic professions. It's only since the 1990s that homosexuality has been out of the World Health Organization classification of mental disorders, and only since the 2000s that sodomy laws were invalidated across the whole of the USA.

Sexology textbooks still ask why people are gay, summarizing various possible evolutionary, genetic, and other biological explanations. There's no equivalent section asking why people are straight.

When did you first decide you were straight?

Isn't it just a phase you may grow out of?

Maybe you just need a good gay lover.

Why do you people have such stereotypical gender roles?

Why do so few of you have stable relationships?

How could the human race survive if everyone were straight, given overpopulation?

✳ QUESTIONS ADAPTED FROM MARTIN ROCHLIN'S HETEROSEXUAL QUESTIONNAIRE

GAY OTHERS

Society demands that gay people explain themselves in ways that straight people don't have to. They have to "come out" because heterosexuality is assumed to be the default. Kids learn that gay people are "different" in a negative way, and bullied for any suggestion they might be gay.

MEDIA REPRESENTATIONS ECHO AND REINFORCE GAY PEOPLE AS OTHER – FROM LACK OF REPRESENTATION AND ACTORS HIDING THEIR SEXUALITIES, TO BEING DEPICTED AS EVIL OR TRAGIC, TO THE NON-THREATENING GAY BEST FRIEND SIDEKICK. GAY PEOPLE ARE NOW ACCEPTABLE IF THEY'RE NOT TOO SEXUAL AND OTHERWISE FIT GENDER AND RELATIONSHIP NORMS. PLOTS STILL OFTEN FOCUSES ON GAYNESS AS THEIR KEY FEATURE.

ACADEMIC & AUTHOR OF POSITIVE IMAGES, **DION KAGAN**

CULTURE & SEXUALITY RESEARCHER **ROGER L. WORTHINGTON**

HOMONEGATIVITY IS BAD FOR STRAIGHT PEOPLE TOO. HETEROSEXUALITY HAS BECOME DEFINED BY WHAT IT ISN'T (GAY), RATHER THAN BY WHAT IT IS. THIS MEANS AN ABSENCE OF A TRUE SENSE OF SEXUAL IDENTITY FOR MANY – PERHAPS MOST – HETEROSEXUAL PEOPLE. IT ALSO INHIBITS CLOSE SAME-GENDER RELATIONSHIPS AND INCREASES PRESSURE TO MARRY AND HAVE SEX TO PROVE THEY'RE "NORMAL".

ROCK HUDSON

NORMAN BATES in PSYCHO

TOM HANKS IN PHILADELPHIA

BUFFY THE VAMPIRE SLAYER

LOVE, SIMON

THE L WORD

ELLEN

INVISIBLE BISEXUALS

A major problem with the straight/gay binary model is that there's no space in it for bisexuals: people who're attracted to more than one gender.

Sexology textbooks still often exclude bisexuality altogether, touch on it briefly before focusing on straight and gay people, or suggest that it doesn't exist or that it's rare.

In 2005 a lab study hit the headlines casting doubt on the existence of bisexual men because it couldn't find any men who got erections in response to both porn involving two men together and porn involving two women together. Improving on the various methodological flaws, later studies did find men who showed bisexual patterns of attraction. In the meantime, the impact of this kind of widely publicized research on men's understanding and experience of their sexuality is huge.

While science is presented as objective, much sexological research is founded on normative assumptions about which sexualities are and aren't up for question, and what kind of evidence is valued.

The binary assumption is embedded in popular culture as well as science. Until recently, characters were represented as going from gay to straight or straight to gay. Those shown in relationships with both men and women were still labelled gay or straight.

PEOPLE TALK ABOUT BROKEBACK MOUNTAIN AS "THE GAY COWBOY MOVIE", BUT ACTUALLY IT'S A BISEXUAL SHEPHERD MOVIE.

INTERESTING HOW BOTH BI MEN AND BI WOMEN ARE ASSUMED TO PREFER MEN REALLY.

FRANK UNDERWOOD, HOUSE OF CARDS

CALLIE TORRES, GREY'S ANATOMY

ROSA DÍAZ, BROOKLYN 99

Bi characters are still often presented as suspicious, manipulative, hypersexual, and dangerous. Fortunately we're getting some better bi representation these days which challenge these stereotypes.

I THINK I MIGHT BE BISEXUAL.

IT'S JUST A PHASE.

MAKE YOUR MIND UP. YOU WANT TO HAVE YOUR CAKE AND EAT IT.

PEOPLE WILL THINK YOU'RE EASY AND JUST DOING IT TO TURN ON YOUR BOYFRIEND.

However, the sexual binary and bi erasure continue to impact bi experience. These common responses – and cultural invisibility – are linked to the higher rates of mental health problems in bi – compared to both gay and straight – people.

SEXUALITY CATEGORIES

The way sexuality is asked on standard forms presents an official sense of what categories are valid, which we internalize. Current good practice in many places for this is something like:

You might notice that this form gets at how people label themselves but not at what they do or feel sexually – which may or may not map onto a label. You may remember from Chapter 1 how these labels wouldn't have made sense at other points in history, and wouldn't work for people in many cultures today.

Each time our sexuality is asked about or measured in this way, it reinforces our understanding that sexuality works in this way. It cements that way of making sense of ourselves, which has a knock-on effect on which experiences feel available to us.

KINSEY AND THE SEXUALITY SPECTRUM

One alternative measurement of sexuality is the famous Kinsey scale. Alfred Kinsey was an American sexologist who did huge studies of male and female sexuality in the 1940s and 50s. The Kinsey Reports revealed that way more people were masturbating and having oral and anal sex and sex before marriage than was assumed at the time.

Although his methods have been criticized, Kinsey's work has been very helpful in demonstrating that we need to think about sexual behaviour, not just identity.

IDENTITY, BEHAVIOUR, ATTRACTION

In addition to sexual identity and behaviour, attraction is an important part of sexuality - whether or not we've acted on it.

A recent survey found that - although only 5.5% of people identified as gay and 2.1% as bisexual - around a quarter of all adults and half of young adults put themselves from 2 to 6 on the Kinsey scale in terms of their attractions (i.e. not exclusively heterosexual).

Rather than being rare or non-existent, bisexual attraction is actually really common. Cultural homophobia and biphobia are at least part of the reason why far fewer people identify in these ways than experience these attractions.

For any aspect of sexuality, more people will experience it than act on it, and more will act on it than identify with it. Of course some will also identify without having acted, and some will act in ways that don't match their attractions (some actors, sex workers, and people learning about their sexuality, for example).

KLEIN AND MULTIPLE SPECTRUMS

Like identity terms, Kinsey type scales only capture our sexual attraction at one point in time – assuming it to be static. Another US sexologist, Fritz Klein, developed Kinsey's idea into a more comprehensive measure of sexuality.

I TRIED TO CAPTURE IDENTITY, BEHAVIOUR, AND ATTRACTION ON MY GRID, AS WELL AS SOCIAL AND POLITICAL IDENTITIES WHICH CAN BE DIFFERENT TOO. AND I INCLUDED THE WAY ALL THESE CAN CHANGE OVER TIME.

FRITZ KLEIN

MY POLITICAL AND SOCIAL IDENTITIES AS A GAY WOMAN ARE IMPORTANT TO ME. AT THE SAME TIME, MY ATTRACTIONS AND FANTASIES DON'T ALWAYS REFLECT THOSE IDENTITIES.

I ENJOY STRONG EMOTIONAL BONDS WITH OTHERS – WITHOUT FEELING SEXUALLY ATTRACTED TO THEM.

The Klein Grid ~

TERMS	MORE THAN 10 YEARS AGO	MORE THAN 5 YEARS AGO	MORE THAN A YEAR AGO	IN THE PAST YEAR	IN THE FUTURE
1 SEXUAL ATTRACTION- who turns you on					
2 SEXUAL BEHAVIOUR- who you have sex with					
3 SEXUAL FANTASIES- who you have sexual fantasies about					
4 EMOTIONAL PREFERENCE- who you have strong emotional bonds with					
5 SOCIAL PREFERENCE- who you like to spend your leisure time with					
6 LIFESTYLE- the sexual identity of the people you spend time with					
7 SEXUAL IDENTITY- how you self identify					
8 POLITICAL IDENTITY- who you identify with					

SCALE USED FOR ROWS 1-5: 1 = OTHER SEX ONLY, 2 = OTHER SEX MOSTLY, 3 = OTHER SEX SOMEWHAT MORE, 4 = BOTH SEXES EQUALLY, 5 = SAME SEX SOMEWHAT MORE, 6 = SAME SEX MOSTLY, 7 = SAME SEX ONLY, 0 = DOES NOT APPLY
SCALE USED FOR ROWS 6-8: 1 = HETEROSEXUAL ONLY, 2 = HETEROSEXUAL MOSTLY, 3 = BISEXUAL MOSTLY, SOME HETERO, 4 = BISEXUAL ONLY, 5 = BISEXUAL MOSTLY, SOME HOMO, 6 = HOMOSEXUAL MOSTLY, 7 = HOMOSEXUAL ONLY

However, any scale from homosexual to heterosexual implicitly suggests that as a person's attraction to the "same gender" decreases, their attraction to the "opposite gender" increases, and vice versa. It's like assuming that people who like coffee more like tea less, and vice versa.

SEXUAL FLUIDITY

Klein's idea that sexuality often shifted over time got very little attention back in the 1980s. The assumption was that sexuality was a fixed, essential part of who we are. The "born this way" narrative seemed a vital counter to prevailing views that being gay was a "lifestyle choice" which people could – and should not – choose.

Recent researchers have returned to sexual fluidity. Lisa Diamond observed that around 2/3 of same-gender-attracted women shift their sexual identity labels, often influenced by the gender of who they were in a relationship with. Jane Ward found that straight-identified men often had sexual encounters with other men, especially in gender-segregated environments. Nigel Dixon found 1/3 of same-gender-attracted men and 2/3 of women reported a shift in attraction over 5 years.

Our sexual identities, behaviours, and attractions can all shift over time. Different experiences can open up different desires and attractions as well as which identities feel like the best fit.

This doesn't mean that we can change our sexualities at will or should be made to try – as in the unethical practice of conversion therapy. Plus, research demonstrates that it doesn't work.

THE FOCUS ON GENDER OF ATTRACTION

You may have noticed that the models of sexual orientation we've considered focus exclusively on gender: ours and the gender that we find attractive. They also generally assume that gender is binary: whether we're attracted to the "same gender" and/or the "opposite gender". What's wrong with this?*

1. THERE ARE LOTS OF DIFFERENT ASPECTS OF GENDER. WHEN WE TALK ABOUT "SAME" OR "OPPOSITE" GENDER ARE WE TALKING ABOUT THE GENDER A PERSON WAS ASSIGNED AT BIRTH? WHAT THEIR BODY AND/OR GENITALS LOOK LIKE NOW? HOW THEY IDENTIFY AS WOMAN, MAN, OR NON-BINARY? OR HOW THEY EXPRESS THEMSELVES IN RELATION TO MASCULINITY AND/OR FEMININITY?

2. NONE OF THESE THINGS IS BINARY. MANY BODIES AND BRAINS DON'T FIT CULTURAL ASSUMPTIONS ABOUT WHAT IT MEANS TO BE "MALE" OR "FEMALE". OVER A THIRD OF PEOPLE EXPERIENCE THEMSELVES AS TO SOME EXTENT THE OTHER, NEITHER, OR BOTH GENDERS.

3. GENDER IS INTERSECTIONAL – WE CAN'T TEASE IT APART FROM RACE, CLASS, DISABILITY, SEXUALITY, AGE, AND MANY OTHER ASPECTS OF A PERSON.

* If you want to know more about these ideas check out our *Gender: A Graphic Guide.*

WHY GENDER OF ATTRACTION ANYWAY?

So, same/opposite-gender models of sexuality don't work for people whose gender – and/or the gender they're attracted to – doesn't fit the binary. They also assume that the most important aspect of a person's sexuality – indeed the aspect that defines them – is the gender they're attracted to.

Think about your own sexual attractions, desires, and identities if you have them. Is gender the most important feature? What about other characteristics?

MANY PEOPLE DESCRIBE BEING BI AS BEING ATTRACTED TO PEOPLE "REGARDLESS OF GENDER", WHILE FOR OTHERS GENDER IS AN IMPORTANT FEATURE. SOME EMPHASIZE THINGS LIKE THE IMPORTANCE OF BELONGING TO A SOCIAL GROUP AND BEING ABLE TO "BE THEMSELVES" OVER SPECIFIC ATTRACTIONS.

SEXUALITY SCHOLAR
HELEN BOWES-CATTON

FOR QUEER PEOPLE OF COLOUR THE SHARED EXPERIENCE OF BEING QUEERLY RACED DUE TO WHITE-HETERO-NORMATIVITY IS HUGELY IMPORTANT. RELATIONSHIPS AND SPACES OF AFFIRMATION AND RECOGNITION ARE VITAL GIVEN THE RACISM, EXCLUSION, AND INVISIBILITY OR HYPERVISIBILITY EXPERIENCED ELSEWHERE.

PSYCHOLOGIST
DR. STEPHANIE DAVIS

Online messaging and gaming, cybersex, and dating and hook-up apps mean that many people experience attractions based on conversations and exchanges that are separate to their offline body or gender.

BLACK MIRROR EPISODE "STRIKING VIPERS"

"THERE'S NO SPARK - NOPE, NOTHING"

SEXUAL CONFIGURATION THEORY [SCT]

Neuroendocrinologist and sex researcher, Sari van Anders, wanted to come up with a theory that decentred gender of attraction and made space for other elements, as well as for the various kinds of attraction we experience, and fluidity over time.

In each possible dimension of sexuality, we may differ in our preferences in solo sex or partnered sex.

MOST OF MY MASTURBATION FANTASIES ARE ABOUT WOMEN, WHEREAS THE SEX I HAVE WITH ANOTHER PERSON IS WITH A MAN.

I GENERALLY EXPERIENCE NURTURING ATTRACTION BUT NOT EROTIC ATTRACTION.

ATTRACTION

IDENTITY

BEHAVIOUR

IN MY MODEL, "EROTICISM" REFERS TO ASPECTS OF SEXUALITY CONNECTED TO PLEASURE, FEELINGS OF AROUSAL, GETTING EXCITED, LUST, ORGASMS, AND SO ON. "NURTURANCE" REFERS TO INTIMACY AND FEELINGS OF LOVE AND CLOSENESS.

There might also be differences in who we're drawn to – and how – erotically and romantically. Of course, we may experience similarities in these areas as well as differences.

SARI VAN ANDERS

Sari includes multiple dimensions of sexuality with SCT. In addition to both the number and gender of partners you like to have, she also considers how strong these attractions are at a particular time, how broad or narrow (like having a specific "type" or not), and whether or not it meshes with cultural norms.

HUH. I'D LOVE TO BE ABLE TO HAVE DIFFERENT PARTNERS FOR DIFFERENT KINDS OF SEX AND RELATIONSHIPS.

We might also think about:
- Levels of sexual attraction (from none to high)
- Physical aspects of attraction that aren't related to gender (e.g. smile, hairstyle, body shape & size)
- Individual characteristics like humour, intelligence, kindness, or extroversion
- The age or life experience of people we're attracted to

AS A BLACK WOMAN, A PARTNER WHO'S A PERSON OF COLOUR AND GETS WHAT THAT'S LIKE IS REALLY IMPORTANT TO ME.

- Whether our sexuality is linked to power dynamics, and whether we like to be dominant, submissive, both or neither
- Roles we like to play (e.g. active or passive, initiating or receiving)
- The kinds of sensations, fantasies, & experiences we enjoy

WHY IDENTITY?

Increasing recognition of sexuality as multidimensional has led to a proliferation of sexual identity terms.

The invention of sexuality as an identity meant individuals could be criminalized, imprisoned, and pathologized on the basis of their sexuality, but also opened the door to fighting for rights on the basis of sexual identity, following feminist and civil rights movements.

Labels help people make sense of their attractions, feel legitimate, find communities of support, and fight for rights. However, labels can also produce more discrimination, as well as making people feel they have to act in certain ways to fit new norms, constraining them to a fixed identity rather than an ever-shifting experience. It's worth seeing the value of labels and holding them lightly.

IDENTITY POLITICS AND QUEER THEORY

As well as questioning binary models of sexuality and gender, **queer theory** and **queer activism** have challenged the idea that people have a sexual (or gender) identity, and that rights should be based on this.

IDENTITY IS NOT A BUNCH OF LITTLE CUBBYHOLES. IT FLOWS BETWEEN, OVER, ASPECTS OF A PERSON. IT'S A RIVER: A PROCESS.

QUEER THEORIST
GLORIA ANZALDUA

Identity politics focuses on gaining inclusion to the existing social order, rather than challenging it and helping those who remain marginalized by it. It can also focus on one axis of oppression personally relevant to us and our group rather than to all. There are many good reasons for resisting Western sexual categorization based on object choice. However, as Cathy Cohen points out, queer perspectives which call for the elimination of categories can ignore how vital social identities and communalties can be for survival.

I REPRESENT THOSE WHO DON'T EVEN WANT TO BE NORMAL; THEY EMBRACE THE THINGS THAT MAKE THEM UNIQUE.

RETURNING TO OUR ASSUMPTIONS

Let's reassess the popular assumptions about sexuality we heard at the beginning of this chapter:

SEXUALITY IS BINARY: YOU'RE STRAIGHT OR YOU'RE GAY

WE ALL HAVE A SEXUAL IDENTITY

THIS IDENTITY IS FIXED

SEXUALITY IS ALL ABOUT OUR GENDER AND THE GENDER WE'RE ATTRACTED TO.

NOPE, MANY PEOPLE ARE ATTRACTED TO MORE THAN ONE GENDER.

NOT EVERYONE. WE MIGHT IDENTIFY IN CERTAIN WAYS WHICH MAY OR MAY NOT MAP ONTO OUR BEHAVIOUR, DESIRES AND ATTRACTIONS.

NO, ALL THESE THINGS CAN CHANGE OVER TIME.

NO, WE EACH HAVE A UNIQUE CONFIGURATION BASED ON ALL KINDS OF POSSIBLE EROTIC OR INTIMATE CONNECTIONS WITH OURSELVES OR OTHERS.

HETEROSEXUALITY IS A LINE WE'RE ORIENTATED AROUND AND ALSO DIRECTED TOWARDS. THE HETEROSEXUAL COUPLE IS SOMETHING WORKED FOR THROUGH THE REPETITION OF TREADING THE LINE OF HETEROSEXUALITY. THOSE WHO FAIL TO STAY ON THE LINE MAY FIND THEMSELVES DISORIENTATED.

QUEER THEORIST & AUTHOR OF *QUEER PHENOMENOLOGY*, SARA AHMED

CHAPTER 4: THE SEX ACT

In his workshops, writer and mental health activist Sascha Altman DuBrul invites participants to reflect on the following question:

THE EROTIC

How is "feeling alive" relevant to sexuality in the sense of what we do sexually?

Audre Lorde describes "the erotic" as this kind of feeling of aliveness. The erotic feeling is what sexual contact with ourselves and other people – as well as many other experiences – can elicit in us.

THERE IS, FOR ME, NO DIFFERENCE BETWEEN WRITING A GOOD POEM AND MOVING INTO SUNLIGHT AGAINST THE BODY OF A WOMAN I LOVE.

AUDRE LORDE

When we think about sexuality, we could be exploring this sense of the erotic, and all of the activities that arouse it, perhaps wondering about which ones we even label as "sex" and why.

Sex could become one practice for finding this sense of aliveness, creativity, and connection with others in our wider lives. And we could invite what we learn about that feeling elsewhere back into sex.

Tuning into whether we're feeling the erotic would be a great way to ensure consent with ourselves and others (more in Chapter 7).

WHAT IS SEX?

When you hear phrases like "the sex act", "having sex", or "sexual intercourse", it's unlikely that you associate them with the acts that make you feel most alive. If you're like most people, you probably don't even think of the activities that make you feel the most horny or turned on (if you experience this). Instead, what you probably think of is:

Sex manuals focus predominantly – often exclusively – on different ways to have this kind of sex. They relegate other forms of sex to foreplay or practice for the "real thing" (e.g. oral sex, solo sex), or to add-ons to the "real thing" to spice it up (e.g. kinky activities or sex toys). PIV intercourse is always central.

In this chapter we'll explore how we got to this understanding of what sex is and what it's for. We'll see how current scientific, medical, and therapeutic understandings of sexual disorders or dysfunctions perpetuate this view. We'll look at the impact on both those who are excluded from and included in this understanding of sex.

THANKS A LOT, SIGMUND

In addition to the mature object of sex being the "opposite sex", Freud theorized that the mature aim of sex was entirely focused on the genitals.

From this we get the idea that sex involving other parts of the body is inferior to sex involving genitals in contact. We also get the fear that the kinds of sex we're into reveal us as having fundamental character flaws.

CHILDREN GO THROUGH A SERIES OF STAGES WHERE THEY ARE EROTICALLY FOCUSED ON OTHER PARTS OF THE BODY BEFORE FOCUSING ON THE GENITALS. AS WITH THE SEXUAL OBJECT, THESE STAGES ARE LINKED TO BEING A CERTAIN KIND OF PERSON. ORALLY FIXATED PEOPLE ARE NAIVE, AND ANALLY RETENTIVE PEOPLE ARE UPTIGHT, FOR EXAMPLE.

Freud also considered any kind of manual stimulation of the genitals - by yourself or another person - to be immature. He believed healthy people would orgasm from penetration, and that "vaginal orgasms" were superior to clitoral ones. We now know these are no different because the - much larger - internal part of the clitoris extends around the vagina.

THE MASTERS OF SEX

William Masters and Virginia Johnson were US sexologists working after Kinsey. Perhaps because of the controversies surrounding Kinsey's work, they studied "normal sex" rather than the diversity of sexualities and sexual practices. They used observation rather than relying on people to report on their sexual experience, and focused on what was happening physiologically rather than exploring how sex related to the rest of a person's life.

Focusing their observations on heterosexual couples having PIV sex meant that their findings inevitably reinforced the view that this is what sex is.

From their observations, Masters and Johnson came up with the **sexual response cycle**: a kind of script of the stages sex should follow, how long these stages should take, and how our bodies should respond at each stage.

This opened the door to the idea that not following this script could be regarded as disordered or dysfunctional.

THE SEXUAL DYSFUNCTIONS

Sexologist Helen Singer Kaplan's revised model became the blueprint for sexual disorders, or dysfunctions, as categorized by the American Psychiatric Association's Diagnostic and Statistical Manual (DSM) which medics and sex therapists use to diagnose people. The World Health Organization's International Classification of Diseases (ICD) includes similar categories.

We'll look at the DSM again, and its section on "paraphilic disorders", in the next chapter. Between these sections, the DSM gives a clear – limited – sense of what counts as normal, functional sex and what doesn't.

"FUNCTIONAL SEX"

The implication of universal human sexual response models, and the diagnostic criteria that draw on these, is that sex should follow a linear progression to orgasm via penis-in-vagina (PIV) sex.

If PIV weren't seen as essential for sex, there wouldn't need to be categories for penetration disorder (where vaginas experience too much pain or tension for penetration) or premature ejaculation (premature for what?).

The fact that there's no female equivalent of premature ejaculation is telling because women orgasming before penetration doesn't interfere with PIV, so it's not seen as important.

National surveys find that over half of the adult population report having at least one "sexual dysfunction". In the past few decades there has been a huge focus on finding drug treatments and other physiological solutions to these "dysfunctions". Would this be the case if different models for human sexual activity had developed instead?

THE DANGER OF UNIVERSALIZING MODELS, PSYCHIATRIC CATEGORIES, AND MEDICAL TREATMENTS IN THIS AREA IS THAT THEY PRESENT A VENEER OF SCIENTIFIC OBJECTIVITY THAT OBSCURES SOMETHING THAT'S ACTUALLY INTENSELY POLITICAL AND VALUE-LADEN.

PSYCHIATRIST & AUTHOR OF SEXUALITY: A BIOPSYCHOSOCIAL APPROACH, CHESS DENMAN

DSM SCIENTIFIC OBJECTIVITY

OBJECTIVITY?! YEAH, RIGHT.

WHO DO THESE MODELS EXCLUDE AND WHAT ARE THE CONSEQUENCES?

The model of functional sex excludes anybody who doesn't engage in sexual activities or experience desire/arousal, and anybody whose main sexual activities don't involve PIV sex and/or orgasm. It also excludes couples whose combined genitals are two penises or two vulvas, or anybody whose body doesn't fit the standard understanding of "male" or "female" genitals.

If the types of sex most common in LGBTQI+ communities were regarded as "functional" sex, we might see different categories of disorder, such as:
- Gag reflex dysfunction
- Anal penetration disorder
- Repetitive strain injury.

Homosexuality may not be listed as a disorder anymore, but the sexual dysfunctions demonstrate that hetero-sex, and by implication straight people, are still regarded as normal. The existence of a heteronormative script also means that LGBTQI+ communities often develop their own, just as limiting, scripts of what is expected to happen during sex.

SAME OLD SCRIPT ...

MEN WHO HAVE SEX WITH MEN CAN FEEL THEY SHOULD HAVE ANAL SEX, AND ASSUMPTIONS ARE PASSED OVER FROM HETERO SEX THAT THE "BOTTOM" (WHO IS PENETRATED) IS MORE FEMININE, SUBMISSIVE, OR GAY THAN THE "TOP".

DOCTOR & AUTHOR OF *STANDING ON HIS SHOULDERS*, DAVID MALEBRANCHE

HOW DOES THIS AFFECT THOSE THE MODEL INCLUDES?

The idea that PIV sex is the normal, functional kind of sex is also bad for people who can have PIV. First, it carries a far greater risk of pregnancy and sexually transmitted infections than many other forms of sex. Also, many people enjoy other forms of sex more but feel they have to default to PIV. Many bodies experience pleasure as much – or more – in areas that are not the penis/vulva.

OVER 3/4 OF WOMEN NEED SOME KIND OF EXTERNAL CLITORAL STIMULATION TO ORGASM. OTHER FORMS OF SEX THAN PIV ARE OFTEN BETTER FOR THIS. 90% OF WOMEN DON'T INCLUDE PENETRATION IN SOLO SEX.

SEXOLOGIST & AUTHOR OF *I AM SEX*, TAMARA GRIFFIN

PIV CAN BE DIFFICULT OR PAINFUL FOR PEOPLE, YET MANY DISABLED PEOPLE ARE TOLD TO GIVE UP ON SEX RATHER THAN TO EXPLORE OTHER FORMS OF SEX.

QUEER THEORIST & EDITOR OF *SEX AND DISABILITY*, ROBERT McRUER

CAN WE GO OFF-SCRIPT YET? I AM <u>SO</u> NOT ENJOYING THIS.

Having one script means that people easily default to this rather than checking out what they – and others – actually want, making unwanted and non-consensual sex more likely.

GENDER AND SEX

Feminists have pointed out that the sexual script is also gendered. It denies women both pleasure and agency.

The idea of "delayed ejaculation" suggests that men's orgasm and ejaculation is vital for sex, whereas women's is not. The language around PIV reinforces this focus on male pleasure and agency. Why do we call PIV "penetrative sex" when "enveloping sex" would be equally accurate?

Many women struggle to identify what turns them on because their pleasure is so de-centred in the (hetero)sexual script. This is linked to wider pressures on women to be "for-others" rather than "for-themselves".

The sexual script isn't great for men either.

MEN ARE EXPECTED TO ACT LIKE UNEMOTIONAL MACHINES WHO ARE EVER READY, WILLING AND ABLE FOR SEX, AND FOCUSED ON THEIR PERFORMANCE. THE IDEA OF SOFT PENISES AS A FAILURE FOR MEN LINKS TO WIDER STEREOTYPES OF MASCULINITY WHICH ARE BAD FOR MEN: NOT BEING SOFT, GENTLE, OR OPEN ABOUT THEIR FEELINGS.

RESEARCHER & AUTHOR OF *THE SCIENCE/FICTION OF SEX, ANNIE POTTS*

THE SEXUAL IMPERATIVE

The normative model of sex contains another major underlying assumption: that sex (genital, orgasmic) is necessary, or imperative. Sexuality scholar Kristina Gupta writes about this imperative in her book *Medical Entanglements*.

The SEXUAL IMPERATIVE ~ or compulsory sexuality ~ includes the beliefs that:
- SEXUAL RELATIONSHIPS ARE THE MOST PRIVILEGED WAYS OF RELATING.
- SEXUALITY AND SELFHOOD are intentwined.
- SEX IS HEALTHY.

We see these ideas throughout sex advice books, which frequently claim things like:

OUR SEXUALITY IS PART OF OUR SOUL OR IDENTITY

"SEXLESS" RELATIONSHIPS WILL INEVITABLY END.

SEX IS THE glue THAT HOLDS RELATIONSHIPS TOGETHER

SEX IS A NATURAL HUMAN NEED, LIKE EATING OR BREATHING

REGULAR SEX IS VITAL FOR MENTAL & PHYSICAL HEALTH AND A COMMITTED RELATIONSHIP

SEX AND SEXUALITY ARE CENTRAL IN OUR CULTURE, AND WE'VE COME TO ORGANIZE OUR PRACTICES OF JOY AND LOVING, LIFE AND FULFILLMENT – AS WELL AS INSTITUTIONAL STRUCTURES – AROUND CONCEPTUALIZATIONS OF THE SEXUAL IMPERATIVE.

FEMINIST RESEARCHER & AUTHOR OF ASEXUAL EROTICS, ELA PRZYBYLO

ASEXUALITY

Asexual – or ace – communities radically challenge the sexual imperative, demonstrating that it's perfectly possible to be a healthy human being – and to have good relationships – without being sexual.

> DUE TO CLEAR EVIDENCE, THE MOST RECENT VERSION OF THE DSM MADE IT CLEAR THAT ASEXUAL PEOPLE SHOULD NOT BE DIAGNOSED AS DISORDERED, AND GOOD PRACTICE GUIDELINES STATE THAT THERAPISTS SHOULD NEVER "TREAT" ASEXUALITY.

PSYCHOLOGIST **LORI BROTTO**

> STILL, STIGMATIZING VIEWS OF ASEXUAL PEOPLE PERSIST, WITH MANY BEING TOLD BY FRIENDS AND PROFESSIONALS THAT IT'S JUST A PHASE OR THEY NEED TO BE CURED.

SEXUALITY SCHOLAR **CJ DeLuzio Chasin**

Instead, we could all learn from people on the asexual spectrum that:

- It's fine not to feel sexual attraction or desire, some or all of the time.
- We can experience sexual and romantic attractions for different people, or can experience one type of attraction without the other, or neither (see pp. 49 and 104).
- It's okay to only experience sexual attraction under certain conditions, such as emotional closeness.

ASEXY AND WE KNOW IT!

SEXUAL DISCREPANCIES AND FLUCTUATION

Part of the sexual imperative is the common idea that everyone should experience the same amount of sexual desire and have sex a certain number of times per week.

This is a pretty weird idea when you think about it. So few aspects of human experience work like this. With most things we're on a spectrum: height, mathematical ability, how outgoing we are, what kind of music we like. Why would sex be so different?

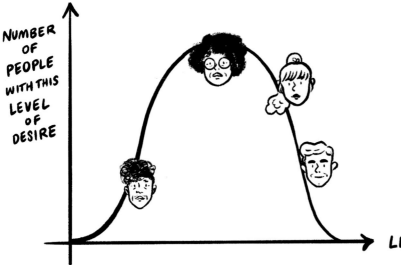

Instead of seeing discrepancies and fluctuations in desire as a problem in relationships, we should expect them as completely normal (more on this in Chapter 5).

FEW RELATIONSHIPS CAN SUSTAIN "HOT" PASSION AT THE SAME TIME AS "WARM" COMPANIONSHIP.

THERAPIST & AUTHOR OF *MATING IN CAPTIVITY*, **ESTHER PEREL**

THE AMOUNT OF SEX PEOPLE HAVE IN LONG-TERM RELATIONSHIPS ISN'T RELATED TO HOW HAPPY THEY ARE IN THEM. MANY VALUE OTHER FORMS OF INTIMACY AND PHYSICAL CLOSENESS MORE.

SOCIOLOGIST & AUTHOR OF *ENDURING LOVE*, **JACQUI GABB**

THE TYRANNY OF NORMAL

There's a cultural sense of the normal sexual orientation people should have, the norm of sexual attractiveness they should aspire to, normal erotic desires they should experience, and normal sexual relationships they should have. We've seen here that we're also taught to aspire to a "normal" type and frequency of sex.

THERAPIST & CREATOR OF *THE ATLAS OF ~~3~~TIC ANATOMY & AROUSAL*, CYNDI DARNELL

ONE OF THE MOST COMMON QUESTIONS I'M ASKED IS "AM I NORMAL?" BUT IF YOU ENJOY WHAT YOU'RE DOING, AND IT'S WHAT EVERYONE INVOLVED WANTS, THEN THIS IS YOUR NORMAL.

Recently, the increasing sense that we should be having, and providing, great and exciting sex – without straying into "abnormal" sex – has made it even more complex. We'll pick this up in the next chapter.

WOMEN OFTEN FEEL THEY CAN'T SPEAK UP WHEN THEY'RE IN PAIN DURING SEX. THEY FEEL EMBARRASSED THERE MIGHT BE SOMETHING WRONG WITH THEM, AND RESPONSIBLE FOR HOW IT WILL IMPACT THEIR PARTNER, MISSING THE FACT THAT IT'S TRIGGERED BY THEIR BODY FEELING UNSAFE.

SEXOLOGIST & INTEGRATIVE THERAPIST, KIM LOLIYA

PLEASURE-FOCUSED OR GOAL-FOCUSED

Many sexual norms clearly see the goal as having erections, penetration, and orgasms, rather than exploring possibilities for enhancing sexual pleasure.

> I CALL IT THE "DOING IT" THEORY OF SEXUAL NORMALCY AND THE "DIDJA COME?" THEORY OF SEXUAL SATISFACTION.

SEX THERAPIST & AUTHOR OF THE HEART & SOUL OF SEX, GINA OGDEN

> WHILE MAINSTREAM SEXPERTISE NOW CENTRES PLEASURE – HAVING HOTTER, MORE EXCITING, EMPOWERED SEX – IT STILL MOSTLY LIMITS THIS TO ACHIEVING OR IMPROVING ORGASMS.

FEMINIST SOCIOLOGIST LAURA HARVEY

Research finds that young women often fake orgasm to bring an end to unwanted sex. The default sexual script plus the expected emotional work of protecting others' feelings can conspire to deny pleasurable – or even consensual – sex.

Trying to achieve the goal of orgasm actually leads to less pleasure during sex, as well as making orgasm less likely. It's like trying to fall asleep when you have insomnia. Alternative approaches include:

- Being present to each moment of a sexual encounter
- Letting go of any script and continually tuning into what feels good
- Focusing on the journey, with no particular destination
- Expanding our understanding of climax.

THE MEANING OF SEX

Another thing missing from common models of sex is *why* people have it. All sexual experiences – and struggles – have different meanings for different people, depending on their cultural context and personal experiences. For example, an orgasm might mean:

SEX THERAPIST
PEGGY KLEINPLATZ

What does it mean if we respond to such vital communication by trying to force our and others' bodies to conform to the sexual script?

THE FEELING OF SEX: HOW, NOT WHAT

Other people might be looking to escape from their body or to feel in their body, to get distracted, to affirm their relationship, to make the other people feel obliged to them, and more.

The focus in sex therapy and sex advice is usually on what people do sexually, not how they engage with sex. This facilitates the selling of endless products, drugs, treatments, and apps to enable a particular kind of sex and the reaching of a particular goal.

The alternative is to focus on the how of being present during sex, tuning into desires, communicating these, eliciting certain feelings, and connecting with ourselves and others.

OTHER POSSIBLE UNDERSTANDINGS OF SEX

We've looked at problematic common metaphors for sex like scripts and baseball games. How might we improve on these?

A BETTER MODEL WOULD BE PIZZA. YOU EAT IT WHEN YOU FEEL LIKE IT, NOT WHEN THE COACH SAYS YOU SHOULD. YOU EAT IT FOR PLEASURE, NOT TO WIN. YOU HAVE WHATEVER TOPPINGS YOU LIKE BEST: ALWAYS THE SAME OR DIFFERENT EACH TIME. YOU STOP WHEN YOU'RE FULL. YOU CAN HAVE IT ALONE OR WITH OTHERS, AND YOU ALWAYS TALK WITH OTHERS ABOUT WHAT KIND OF PIZZAS YOU'RE GOING TO HAVE BEFORE ORDERING.

SEX EDUCATOR **AL VERNACCHIO**

OR WHAT ABOUT DANCING? IT'S SOMETHING WE LEARN FROM THE WORLD AROUND US. IT HAS MANY DIFFERENT STYLES, WHICH VARY ACROSS CULTURES AND CHANGE OVER THE COURSE OF OUR LIVES. WE HAVE FREE CHOICE OVER THE KIND OF DANCING WE DO, OR WHETHER WE LIKE DANCING AT ALL. IF WE HAVE ANY PROBLEMS WITH DANCING, WE MIGHT PAY FOR LESSONS, LEARN FROM DIFFERENT PEOPLE IN OUR LIVES, OR TRY A NEW KIND OF DANCING.

THERAPIST & AUTHOR OF *SEX IS NOT A NATURAL ACT*, LEONORE TIEFER

DIVERSITY: WHAT IS SEX AGAIN?

If sex was defined more broadly, using one of these new metaphors, would over half of people report sexual difficulties?

WE CAN EXPAND OUR UNDERSTANDING BY LISTING ALL THE ACTIVITIES THAT SOMEBODY MIGHT FIND EROTIC OR SENSUAL. ALL ARE EQUALLY VALID — SO LONG AS WE DO THEM CONSENSUALLY. WE CAN REFLECT ON WHICH WE'D BE A "YES, NO, OR MAYBE" FOR, AND WHAT THEY'D MEAN TO US. WE CAN SHARE LISTS WITH PEOPLE WE MIGHT HAVE SEX WITH TO FIND OUR OVERLAPS.

SEX EDUCATOR & AUTHOR OF ENJOY SEX, JUSTIN HANCOCK

Most people don't have these conversations. Psychologist Sandra Byers found that people who'd been in a relationship for over a decade still only understood about 60% of what their partner liked sexually and only around 20% of what they didn't. People also struggle to share their desires and dislikes when dating or hooking up. There's still a common idea that communicating about sex is unsexy, rather than a potentially very hot way of ensuring both pleasurable and consensual sex.

What would it be like if all forms of sex — and communication about sex — were represented in media, sex advice, porn, and sex ed?

SEX IN ITS CULTURAL CONTEXT

Returning to the theme of how normative sexuality is embedded within patriarchy, colonialism, and capitalism, it is telling that the recognition and treatment of "female sexual dysfunctions" only emerged when women's sexual dissatisfaction became a threat to heterosexual marriage and the nuclear family.

Narrow understandings of sex create the constant anxiety that we are lacking, thus enabling the selling of products.

WE NEED TO ARTICULATE A PRO-SEX, PRO-PLEASURE POLITIC IN THE FACE OF RECALCITRANT AND DEMEANING STEREOTYPES THAT OBJECTIFY, DEHUMANIZE, AND DEVALUE BLACK WOMEN'S BODIES AND LIVES.

THE CRUNK FEMINIST COLLECTIVE

Black, disabled, fat, and trans feminists have pointed out the radical potentials of claiming pleasure in a world where many bodies have historically been denied it.

Just as our experiences of sex often echo the ways we're treated in the wider world, so rethinking sex can open up wider challenges to the way our bodies, desires, lives, and labour our treated.

THE EROTIC IS SO FEARED AND RELEGATED TO THE BEDROOM ALONE BECAUSE ONCE WE BEGIN TO FEEL DEEPLY ALL THE ASPECTS OF OUR LIVES, WE BEGIN TO DEMAND FROM OURSELVES AND OUR LIFE PURSUITS THAT THEY FEEL IN ACCORDANCE WITH THAT JOY WHICH WE KNOW OURSELVES TO BE CAPABLE OF.

AUDRE LORDE

CHAPTER 4: SEXUAL DESIRES AND BEING NORMAL

We've seen that historic scientific understandings of sexuality were bound up in colonialist and capitalist thinking and how this required defining some lives and bodies as more "normal" than others to justify unequal treatment. We've also seen how the project of sexology became to delineate abnormal "deviance" or "perversion" from assumed normal sexual practices.

THIS HAS CONTINUED TO THE PRESENT, DESPITE MY ARGUMENT THAT WE ALL BEGIN POLYMORPHOUSLY PERVERSE...

...AND MY WORK, WHICH FOUND THAT MUCH OF WHAT WAS CONSIDERED ABNORMAL WAS ACTUALLY PRETTY COMMON.

In addition to the sexual dysfunctions, categorizations of mental disorders also include the **paraphilias** (abnormal sexual desires). In this chapter, we'll critique the common assumptions around normal/abnormal sexual desire, such as:

- Determination of normal/ abnormal desire is supported by scientific evidence.
- Most people are normal, and only a few abnormal.
- Normal people are happier and healthier with better sex lives.
- We should all aspire to normal sex.

And we'll ask what we can learn from those who claim sexual desires outside of "normal".

CONCERNING DESIRES

To explore whether this normal/abnormal division is the most helpful way to distinguish desires, let's think about how we would decide which was a cause for concern. Would you be concerned if a friend wanted to act on these desires? Why?

I LOVE BEING PUT IN TERRIFYING SITUATIONS THAT MAKE ME CRY AND SCREAM. I CAN PAY PEOPLE TO PUT ME IN A SPECIAL DEVICE WHICH WILL TAKE ME INTO THAT STATE. I NEVER KNOW QUITE WHAT WILL HAPPEN BEFOREHAND, AND THERE'S NO WAY TO STOP ONCE I START. BUT WHEN IT'S DONE I'LL BEG THEM TO DO IT AGAIN.

MY DESIRE IS FOR A PUBLIC SCENE. I'D SPEND WEEKS PREPARING. I'D DRESS IN TIGHT CLOTHING AND SO WOULD MY MALE PARTNER. OUR AUDIENCE WOULD WATCH US BEAT EACH OTHER, ADMIRING OUR PHYSIQUES. IT CAN RESULT IN PERMANENT DAMAGE, BUT IT'D BE WORTH THE THRILL.

I WANT TO PAY A STRANGER TO CAUSE EXTREME PAIN TO MY GENITAL AREA. IT WON'T CAUSE ANY LONG-LASTING HARM, AND IT'LL MAKE ME FEEL SO ATTRACTIVE AFTERWARDS.

I SOMETIMES MEET WITH A GROUP IN PRIVATE TO WATCH OTHERS ROLEPLAY BEING HUMILIATED, ASSAULTED, AND TORTURED. I ENJOY THOSE EVENINGS A LOT.

* We'll come back to these examples on page 79.

THE SEX HIERARCHY: DRAWING THE LINE

As we saw on page 17, while different cultures over time have used different criteria, they've always tended to delineate acceptable from unacceptable sexual desires. Today, people often use criteria such as:

DOES IT HARM YOU OR SOMEONE ELSE, AND CAUSE TEMPORARY OR PERMANENT DAMAGE?

IS IT A RARE OR COMMON PRACTICE? DOES IT CAUSE PAIN OR PLEASURE?

DOES IT INVOLVE OTHER PEOPLE? ARE THEY KNOWN OR STRANGERS? HOW EXTREME IS IT?

IS IT ILLEGAL? CAN PEOPLE CONSENT TO IT IN AN INFORMED WAY?

Ideal sexual desires

ACCEPTABILITY

PIV SEX IN HETERO COUPLE

ANAL SEX BETWEEN MEN

SOLO SEX

THREESOME

BEING TIED UP AND HURT

GETTING TURNED ON BY OBJECTS

SEEING A SEX WORKER

SEX WITH ANIMALS

Unacceptable sexual desires

You might consider where the practices from page 72 would sit on the current cultural pyramid.

WE HAVE A CULTURAL SEX HIERARCHY, LIKE A PYRAMID OF ACCEPTABILITY. SOMEWHERE ON THIS, SCIENCE, RELIGION, LAW, AND MEDICINE DRAW A LINE WHICH SEPARATES DESIRES THAT ARE SEEN AS NORMAL, HEALTHY, AND GOOD, FROM THOSE SEEN AS ABNORMAL, UNHEALTHY, AND BAD.

GAYLE RUBIN

THE PARAPHILIC DISORDERS

Medical diagnostic manuals are one of the key sources which define and reinforce what a culture regards as normal/abnormal. The DSM-5 defines a paraphilic disorder as "intense and persistent sexual interest other than ... in genital stimulation or preparatory fondling with phenotypically normal, physically mature, consenting human partners". The current list is:

- **VOYEURISTIC DISORDER**
  (enjoying watching other people)
- **EXHIBITIONISTIC DISORDER**
  (enjoying being watched)
- **SEXUAL MASOCHISTIC DISORDER**
  (finding it exciting to be humiliated, tied up, and/or to receive painful stimulation)
- **SEXUAL SADISM DISORDER**
  (finding it exciting to do those kinds of things to another person)
- **FETISHISTIC DISORDER**
  (getting turned on by objects or materials)
- **TRANSVESTIC DISORDER**
  (becoming aroused by wearing clothes usually associated with the "opposite sex")
- **FROTTEURISTIC DISORDER**
  (getting turned on by rubbing up against other people)
- **PEDOPHILIC DISORDER**
  (being sexually attracted to children)

MASOCHISM ☒
EXHIBITIONISM ☒

EXHIBITIONISM ☒
SADISM ☒
MASOCHISM ☒
FETISHISM ☒

☒ VOYEURISM
☒ SADISM

FETISHISM ☒

Up until recently, simply experiencing these desires would class you as having a paraphilia. But with the latest revision to be classed as having a paraphilic disorder you need to: (A) have experienced recurrent or intense arousal from the idea for over 6 months; and (B) experience distress, impairment, or non-consensual behaviour because of it.

DISTRESS AND HARM TO OTHERS

It might seem valid that paraphilias count as "disorders" if they cause distress, but having a sexual desire which is culturally regarded as sick, bad, or wrong causes stigma and discrimination. So many people who experience such desires will likely experience distress around them.

Having your desire listed in the DSM – even with the caveat that it may not cause distress – reinforces the cultural sense that it's unacceptable or abnormal. This was the case for homosexuality in the 1970s, and remains the case for many "kinky" desires now.

It might also seem valid that paraphilias count as "disorders" if they might harm others – as paedophilia would if it was acted upon, or as any of the activities on the list would if acted upon without the consent of the other person.

However, we can question whether it's useful to class acting on a desire non-consensually as a mental disorder, versus belonging in the realm of criminal justice or morality, as it would if someone acted upon a desire to own someone else's property, or to engage in non-consensual PIV sex.

ABNORMAL OR CULTURALLY UNACCEPTABLE?

Many non-sexual activities like these are at least as potentially damaging, painful, and likely to be non-consensual as many of those listed as paraphilias, but they rarely cause concern because they're culturally normative.

Similarly, the activities that happen on the average stag/hen party are often far more risky, non-consensual, and uncontrolled than those at a kink party or club. We could likewise compare play piercing and tattooing, or suspension bondage and rock climbing.

Psychologist and author of *Perverse Psychology*, Jemma Tosh, points out that we can see cultural normativity in the inclusion of transvestic disorder in the DSM. This is almost exclusively diagnosed in men. Why is male femininity pathologized, but not female masculinity?

PROBLEMS WITH THE PARAPHILIAS

The list includes a mixture of desires that are there because they are non-consensual if acted upon, uncommon, or potentially harmful. Many of the desires on the list are on a spectrum with things that apply to a lot of people. Where do we draw the line? And why?

THE PARAPHILIC DISORDERS ARE MUDDLED, UNCLEAR, INCONSISTENT, AND LACK ANY BASIS IN EVIDENCE.

SEXOLOGIST & AUTHOR OF SADOMASOCHISM, CHARLES MOSER

WATCHING BURLESQUE ⟷ VOYEURISM
WEARING SEXY MATERIALS ⟷ FETISHISM
ENJOYING TURNING HEADS ⟷ EXHIBITIONISM
ENJOYING LOVE BITES ⟷ SADOMASOCHISM

HELLO BOYS

wonderbra

TWITTER
@
#metoo
@
#me

Moser points out that culturally normative sexualities can cause distress and impairment just as much as non-normative ones.

BDSM: BONDAGE AND DISCIPLINE, DOMINANCE AND SUBMISSION, AND SADOMASOCHISM

MY RESEARCH IN THE 1950S DEMONSTRATED THAT GAY AND STRAIGHT PEOPLE HAD NO DISCERNABLE DIFFERENCES IN MENTAL HEALTH.

PSYCHOLOGIST EVELYN HOOKER

WHEN WE STUDY THE GENERAL POPULATION, KINKSTERS ARE NO MORE PSYCHOLOGICALLY UNHEALTHY THAN ANYBODY ELSE, AND THEIR CHILDHOODS ARE NO DIFFERENT EITHER.

PSYCHOLOGIST DARREN LANGDRIDGE

Recent research on BDSM challenges popular representations of kinksters with traumatic childhoods.

The huge popularity of *Fifty Shades* of Grey also demonstrates how common kinky desires are: over 1/3 of people use kink equipment, and 2/3 have bondage fantasies. As with sexual attraction, let's remember that more people will experience desires than will either act upon them or identify as kinksters. Kinky people are also no more likely than others to be harmed by their activities, or to be abusive, which isn't to say those things don't happen, but no more than in any other group.

THE STIGMA AROUND KINK IS DANGEROUS BECAUSE IT MEANS PEOPLE ARE LESS LIKELY TO ACCESS GOOD INFORMATION ABOUT HOW TO PRACTICE KINK, OR TO SPEAK UP IF ABUSE DOES HAPPEN BECAUSE OF FEARING BEING HELD RESPONSIBLE FOR DAMAGING THE COMMUNITY.

ACTIVIST KITTY STRYKER

LEARNING FROM KINKSTERS

As with other sexualities deemed abnormal, psychologists, medics, media producers, and journalists have attempted to categorize kinksters and to come up with single, universal explanations for their activities.

However, kink practices are diverse and hold different meanings for people. Instead of looking for a universal explanation, let's consider what we might learn about the erotic from them. Kinksters have come up with useful ways to tune into desires, to communicate them to others, and to navigate acting on them consensually.

I HAVE A HIGH-POWERED JOB, SO I NEED THIS TO LET GO OF CONTROL NOW AND THEN.

KINKSTERS HELP US TO EXPAND OUR EROTIC IMAGINATIONS BEYOND WHAT WE'VE LEARNT TO SEE AS "PROPER SEX", QUESTIONING THE LINES WE DRAW BETWEEN SEX AND PLAY, LEISURE, SPIRITUAL PRACTICE, ART, SPORT, AND MORE.

SEX POSITIVE OR SEX CRITICAL?

With sexualities which are marginalized and pathologized, there's often a tendency for people to fight for their rights in ways that are problematic. For example:

1. Flipping the narrative to suggest the marginalized group is actually superior to others.

2. Arguing that the group is normal in every other way – so should be granted access to normativity – often in comparison to other "less normal" groups.

Kink communities – and other "sex positive" movements – can often present more diverse understandings of the erotic as imperative, just as mainstream sex advice and therapy does with PIV sex.

VANILLA!

MUNDANE

NO-ONE'S REALLY ASEXUAL!

FREE YOUR MIND!

I CAN HEAL YOU...

Any default sexual script will alienate some people and lead to others having unwanted and non-consensual experiences.

AUTHORS OF *FUCKED: ON BEING SEXUALLY DYSFUNCTIONAL IN SEX-POSITIVE QUEER SCENES*

ASEXUAL PEOPLE, SURVIVORS, AND PEOPLE WHO STRUGGLE WITH SEX – OR JUST AREN'T INTO THESE PRACTICES – CAN FEEL PATHOLOGIZED, MARGINALIZED, AND PRESSURED TO DO THINGS THEY DON'T WANT TO DO.

FUCKED
on being sexually dysfunctional in sex-positive queer scenes

WE SHOULD BE EQUALLY CRITICAL IN OUR THINKING AROUND MARGINALIZED AND NORMATIVE DESIRES.

CRITICAL SEXOLOGIST LISA DOWNING

EMBRACING OR CHALLENGING NORMATIVITY?

Studies of US kink communities by ethnographers Staci Newmahr and Margot Weiss find that wider cultural injustices are often present. Kink spaces are overwhelmingly white and middle-class, often inaccessible and alienating to disabled people, working-class people, and people of colour. These spaces often rely upon capitalist expectations of spending money, narrow beauty ideals, and unquestioned heteronormative gendered power dynamics: that, whether submissive or dominant, men's pleasure is central.

MEDIA REPRESENTATIONS OF BDSM PRESENT IT AS ACCEPTABLE IF THE RELATIONSHIP IS OTHERWISE A HETERONORMATIVE COUPLE.

AUTHOR OF *VICARIOUS KINKS*, UMMNI KHAN

FIFTY SHADES FREED

SECRETARY

I COULD SEEK TO PERSUADE THE MAJORITY THAT SADOMASOCHISM ISN'T VIOLENT OR SELF-DESTRUCTIVE. BUT THAT WOULD REQUIRE LITTLE WHITE LIES, EMPHASIZING WHAT S/M HAS IN COMMON WITH VANILLA RATHER THAN WHERE THEY PART COMPANY.

ACTIVIST-WRITER PATRICK CALIFIA

Robin Bauer and Mollena Williams point out the potentials of kink play to reveal injustices and normativities, as well as to reproduce them. People can use kink play to reflect on their privileges and oppressions.

BDSM ENABLES US TO CONSIDER THE COMPLEXITY AND DIVERSENESS OF BLACK WOMEN'S SEXUALITY AND SEXUAL PRACTICE.

AUTHOR OF *THE COLOR OF KINK*, ARIANE CRUZ

SEX ADDICTION

Recent years have seen the invention of the sex addict. Although the evidence for "hypersexual disorder" was deemed too shaky to add it to the DSM-5, therapy for sex addiction has become big business and a major new cultural bogeyman.

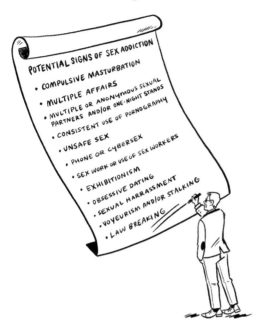

The caveat that these activities don't *necessarily* mean that somebody is a sex addict doesn't prevent the sense that these activities are somehow more prone to being addictive than coupled PIV sex. The list confusingly mixes non-consensual and harmful activities alongside ones which aren't necessarily so, and further stigmatizes already vulnerable groups.

THE GLOBAL MEDICAL MANUAL (ICD-11) INCLUDES THE CATEGORY OF "COMPULSIVE SEXUAL BEHAVIOUR DISORDER", MAKING IT CLEAR THAT IT'S NOT AN "ADDICTION". IT EMPHASIZES THAT THERE IS NO "RIGHT" AMOUNT OR TYPE OF SEX, AND THAT PEOPLE SHOULD NOT BE DIAGNOSED OR TREATED IF THEIR DISTRESS STEMS FROM CULTURAL STIGMA OR A MORAL CONFLICT OF THEIR DESIRES.

HEAD OF **PINK THERAPY**
DOMINIC DAVIES

MANY OF THESE PRACTICES ARE PARTICULARLY COMMON IN GAY COMMUNITIES, SO SEX ADDICTION EASILY BECOMES A NEW WAY OF PATHOLOGIZING HOMOSEXUALITY.

SOCIOLOGIST & AUTHOR OF
DISORDERS OF DESIRE,
JANICE IRVINE

PATHOLOGIZATION OF HIGH AND LOW DESIRE

The concept of sex addiction fits into a broader tradition of pathologizing desire as too high or too low. It defines the amount of sexual desire people should have, the types of desire deemed appropriate, how they should act on these, and what the acceptable reasons are for having sex (e.g. enhancing intimacy with a partner but not alleviating loneliness).

PSYCHIATRISTS AND THERAPISTS SEEM TO BELIEVE THERE'S A GOLDILOCKS AMOUNT OF SEX PEOPLE SHOULD BE HAVING. PROBABLY THE AMOUNT THEY'RE HAVING THEMSELVES.

AUTHOR OF *THE GUIDE TO GETTING IT ON,*
PAUL JOANNIDES

Asexual people and "sex addicts" are pressured to conform to these expectations, particularly if they are in relationships with somebody who conforms better.

However, some groups face recrimination for expressing any sexual desire. Disabled people and people with chronic health conditions are often told by medics to give up on sex. Sex after a certain age is often regarded with disgust and/ or ridicule. Young people and women are heavily policed when it comes to how much desire they should have and how they should express it.

WHAT DO LABELS OPEN UP AND CLOSE DOWN?

As we'll see in Chapter 6, sex addicts can be seen as one of a number of **sexual subjects** who have been invented in recent years through a cultural process by which people learn to make sense of their experiences – and act upon them – in particular ways.

But, of course, many people really do experience problems with their sexual desires and practices, finding that they interfere with their lives, put them at risk, or distress them. It can then be useful to ask what the identity of "sex addict" – or any other identity label – opens up and closes down for people.

IT HELPS ME FEEL THAT THIS IS A REAL THING THAT'S GOING ON FOR ME, THAT IT'S NOT JUST MY FAULT, THAT I'M NOT ALONE, AND THAT I CAN GET SUPPORT. BUT I WORRY PEOPLE WILL LOOK DOWN ON ME IF I SAY I'M A SEX ADDICT, THAT IT MEANS I'LL BE STUCK WITH THAT LABEL FOREVER, AND THAT THERE'LL BE NO UNDERSTANDING OF THE UNIQUENESS OF MY EXPERIENCE OR WHY WHAT I'M DOING IS SO IMPORTANT TO ME.

WORKING WITH TROUBLING DESIRES

It's useful to explore the cultural messages that people struggling with their desires have received about sexual normality and how these inform their sense of having a problem. Instead of trying to stop the desires, it's important to explore what they mean to the person: why they're so compelling.

For example, online sex might be a soothing way to switch off, or a place to find out what turns them on, for example. If people can be present to their desires and experiences, they can also slow down enough to make intentional, ethical choices about whether or not to act upon them.

This is extremely difficult within the wider cultural double bind: consumer capitalism tells us we're entitled to have what we desire and should immediately act on our cravings. But normal/abnormal models of sex create huge shame and stigma around particular desires. People swing from trying to ignore or eradicate the bogeyman of their desires, to mindlessly acting upon these desires, rather than engaging with curiosity and care for themselves and others.

SEX, BODIES, AND POWER

Why have we ended up in a situation where we categorize people as having normal or abnormal sexual desires? Sexuality and mental health are key zones in which we're encouraged to self-monitor, to work on ourselves, to perform being normal. Who benefits from this?

IN A SURVEILLANCE SOCIETY, WE LEARN TO MONITOR AND SCRUTINIZE OURSELVES COMPARED TO WHAT WE'VE BEEN TAUGHT IS "NORMAL". ABNORMALITIES ARE LOCATED INSIDE US, AS FLAWS IN OUR IDENTITY, RATHER THAN PROBLEMS IN THE SYSTEMS AND STRUCTURES AROUND US. WE ENGAGE IN FORMS OF BODILY DISCIPLINE AND TECHNOLOGIES OF THE SELF TO ACHIEVE NORMALITY.

TINDER
UPLOAD PIC
FILL OUT YOUR PROFILE!

VIAGRA

EVERYTHING IN THE WORLD IS ABOUT SEX EXCEPT SEX. SEX IS ABOUT POWER.

A docile population with a strong commitment to conformity means:
- High levels of productivity (generating profit for those in power)
- High levels of purchasing (generating more profit from products that trade on insecurity)
- Low levels of political engagement and resistance to the systems which (re)produce these norms.

THE WORK OF SEX

WORK CULTURE COMES TO SHAPE HOW WE TALK ABOUT SEX. WE HAVE TO HAVE "GREAT SEX", WHICH REQUIRES TRAINING, SKILLS, MANAGEMENT, AND THE INVESTMENT OF TIME AND MONEY.

ROS GILL

The imperative to have sex that is both great and normal leads to even more self-monitoring as people tread the tightrope between being "spicy" enough to be desired and retain long-term relationships, while never falling into abnormal or disordered sex.

WOMEN IN PARTICULAR HAVE TO WALK THE LINE BETWEEN BEING SEEN AS A SLUT OR A PRUDE, AS WELL AS BEING RESPONSIBLE FOR THE LABOUR FOR ENSURING GREAT SEX.

PSYCHOLOGIST & AUTHOR OF ORGASMIC BODIES, HANNAH FRITH

All the time the lines on the sex hierarchy shift; sex acts that were once unacceptable become acceptable. We have to keep up without falling into the wrong side. This is not to say that engaging effortfully and consciously in sex is a problem, but the version of sexual entrepreneurship that we're sold is about meeting an ever-changing goal of great sex and desirability. It's not about doing the things that would enable us to be more present and engaged with the erotic desires and experiences we have.

ALTERNATIVES TO BINARIES AND HIERARCHIES

In the last 3 chapters, we've seen that people can't be divided into binaries on any aspect of sexuality:
- Majority and minority sexual orientations
- Functional and dysfunctional sexual bodies
- Normal and abnormal sexual desires.

Attempts to do so are bad for those who are put in both the inferior and superior categories. As we saw on page 83, the answer is neither to claim a place for your particular identity within the norm, nor to flip the hierarchy so that you're now at the top.

GAY RIGHTS HAVE OFTEN BEEN FOUGHT FOR ON THE BASIS OF GAY PEOPLE BEING OTHERWISE NORMAL (GOOD CITIZENS WANTING MARRIAGE AND CHILDREN): DISTANCING FROM LESS NORMATIVE QUEERS. SIMILARLY BISEXUAL RIGHTS OFTEN REST ON "MYTH-BUSTING": WE'RE NOT CONFUSED, NOT PROMISCUOUS, NOT NON-MONOGAMOUS, NOT GOING THROUGH A PHASE. BUT THAT SUGGESTS THERE'S SOMETHING WRONG WITH UNCERTAINTY, BEING SEXUALLY ACTIVE OR NON-MONOGAMOUS, OR SEXUALITY BEING FLUID.

ACTIVIST & AUTHOR OF *BI*, SHIRI EISNER

I'M STARTING TO EMBRACE THE FACT THAT SEXUALITY IS SO OFTEN UNCERTAIN OR CHANGEABLE – AND FULL OF POSSIBILITIES.

BENIGN DIVERSITY

> MOST PEOPLE FIND IT DIFFICULT TO GRASP THAT THEIR MOST TREASURED SEXUAL DELIGHT WILL BE THOROUGHLY REPULSIVE TO SOMEONE ELSE, AND VICE VERSA. MOST PEOPLE MISTAKE THEIR SEXUAL PREFERENCES FOR A UNIVERSAL SYSTEM THAT WILL OR SHOULD WORK FOR EVERYONE.

GAYLE RUBIN

An alternative model to the old sex hierarchies is that of benign diversity: regarding all forms of sexuality as equally valid and acceptable, regardless of how common, extreme, or culturally acceptable they are.

This might allow us to stop treating unaroused, non-orgasmic bodies and anxieties around being abnormal, and instead to treat the root cause: our problematic cultural understandings of sex and the systems of power underlying them (heteronormativity, patriarchy, colonialism, white supremacy, capitalism, etc.).

> JUST AS A WORLD DESIGNED FOR CERTAIN BODIES LITERALLY DISABLES MANY OF US, SO THE CULTURAL UNDERSTANDING OF SEX – AND THE SCIENCE AND MEDICINE FOUNDED ON THIS – EMOTIONALLY DISORDERS US.

THERAPIST & AUTHOR OF *LIFE ISN'T BINARY*, **ALEX IANTAFFI**

THE ETHICS OF SEX

Does benign diversity mean anything goes: that we'd make no distinctions between different forms of sex? Not necessarily. Arguably the focus on normal/abnormal distinctions has detracted from the far more important distinction we could make between ethical and unethical sexual behaviours.

> IT DOESN'T MATTER HOW SOCIALLY TRANSGRESSIVE A DESIRE IS, THE QUESTION SHOULD BE WHETHER IT HAS BEEN ACTED UPON COERCIVELY OR NOT. THAT'S THE REALM OF JUSTICE, NOT MENTAL HEALTH.

CHESS DENMAN

> LIKE SEX ADDICTION, THERE HAVE BEEN REPEATED ATTEMPTS TO ADD "PARAPHILIC COERCIVE DISORDER" (DESIRE TO RAPE) TO THE DSM. WHAT WOULD BE THE IMPACT OF FRAMING AN ALREADY VASTLY UNDERREPORTED AND UNDER-CONVICTED CRIME AS A MENTAL DISORDER?

JEMMA TOSH

> LABELING SEX ADDICTION A DISORDER HAS WRESTED RESPONSIBILITY AWAY FROM PHILANDERING MEN BY MAKING IT SEEM OUT OF THEIR CONTROL.

AUTHOR OF THE MYTH OF SEX ADDICTION, DAVID LEY

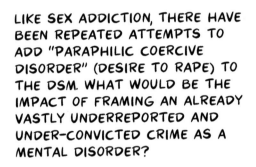

Removing stigma and shame around sexual desires could help people to look at them with openness and curiosity, determining which they could act on ethically and which not, exploring alternatives such as fantasy, roleplay, and meeting those desires in other ways.

RETURNING TO OUR ASSUMPTIONS

In addition to exploring individual sexual ethics in far more depth, we could look at the ethics of various industries which promote limited understandings of sexuality. The toll this has taken over the years in terms of human suffering - and even death - is huge.

SEXUAL AROUSAL <u>CAN</u> OCCUR FROM ANYTHING UNDER THE SUN, INCLUDING THE SUN.

PROFESSOR OF FORENSIC MEDICINE & AUTHOR OF *NECROPHILIA*, ANIL AGGRAWAL

AND YET HUMANS CONTINUE TO BE THE ONLY CREATURES THAT STIGMATIZE, PUNISH AND CREATE SHAME AROUND THEIR SEXUAL DESIRES.

HISTORIAN & AUTHOR OF *A CURIOUS HISTORY OF SEX*, KATE LISTER

Let's revise the assumptions from the start of the chapter:

- NORMAL/ABNORMAL DISTINCTIONS COULD BE REPLACED BY BENIGN DIVERSITY
- CLASSIFICATIONS ARE CLEARLY HIGHLY RELATED TO CURRENT CULTURAL NORMS AND RESULT IN UNNECESSARY STIGMA AND SHAME
- MOST PEOPLE HAVE SOME OF WHAT HAVE BEEN CLASSED "ABNORMAL" DESIRES
- THOSE ASSUMED TO BE DISORDERED ARE NO DIFFERENT, AND NO LESS HEALTHY, THAN ANYONE ELSE.
- PERHAPS THOSE WHO HAVE MOST TO TEACH US ABOUT SEX ARE THOSE IN THE CULTURAL MARGINS - ALTHOUGH THIS DOESN'T MEAN FLIPPING THE SEX HIERARCHY, AS THAT CAN BE EQUALLY PROBLEMATIC

CHAPTER 5: EROTIC RELATIONSHIPS AND EXPRESSING SEXUALITY

So far we've explored sexuality in relation to: how we identify based on who we're attracted to; the kind of sex we have; and our sexual desires. In this chapter, we'll consider the different contexts and relationships in which we express our sexuality. We've seen that the ways we express our sexuality – in terms of the erotic relationships we form and the sexual activities we engage in there – may or may not mesh with our actual erotic desires and sexual attractions.

People may deny some of their attractions and desires, and form normative relationships, in order to fit in.

They may follow sexual scripts rather than admitting what really turns them on because of the normal/abnormal distinction. Or they may feel pressured to be sexual because of the sexual imperative.

These repressions of our sexuality are linked to heteronormative expectations of gender roles, opposite sex attraction, PIV sex, and monogamous coupledom.

THE GOLD STANDARD: MONOGAMOUS COUPLEDOM

The strong message from wider culture is that the most – sometimes only – appropriate place to express our sexuality is within a romantic, monogamous, long-term coupled relationship. From dating apps to romantic comedies, the emphasis is on finding The One: the perfect partner with whom you will fall in love and have great sex forever.

Sex and relationship therapy and advice largely focuses on enabling couples to maintain sexual relationships with each other, rather than exploring other options to meet their erotic desires. Having sex with others is presented as dangerous to the couple unit, so couples are encouraged to find other ways of acting on any such fantasies. Having sex alone is generally presented as a way of practicing for the "real thing", at risk of becoming addictive or paraphilic if it becomes pleasurable in its own right. We'll return to solo sex at the end of the chapter.

SEX ADVICE FOR DUMMIES

A THREESOME IS A COMMON FANTASY, BUT ACTING ON THIS WOULD JEOPARDIZE YOUR RELATIONSHIP. INSTEAD, TRY HAVING SEX IN FRONT OF A MIRROR.

THAT SOUNDS LIKE MORE OF A FOURSOME THAN A THREESOME.

AND STRANGELY TWO-DIMENSIONAL AND UNIMAGINATIVE.

MONONORMATIVITY

Linked to heteronormativity, mononormativity is the sense that monogamy is the normal, natural, morally superior way of doing relationships. The love triangle plot rests on the tension of mononormativity and characters resisting or resolving their desire for more than one person so as to achieve monogamy. This is so prevalent and taken for granted that much current fiction would collapse without it.

SO DO I.

NO PROBLEM.

I LOVE YOU.

The End!

MARRIAGE AS A MONOGAMOUS LOVE RELATIONSHIP IS ACTUALLY PRETTY NEW. IT'S ONLY SINCE THE 1950S THAT THE MAJORITY OF PEOPLE COULD AFFORD TO MARRY FOR LOVE AND PERSONAL CHOICE.

HISTORIAN & AUTHOR OF MARRIAGE: A HISTORY, STEPHANIE COONTZ

LOVE BECAME THE NEW RELIGION, WITH PEOPLE LOOKING TO PARTNERS TO FULFILL NEEDS WHICH MIGHT PREVIOUSLY HAVE BEEN MET BY A COMMUNITY OR FAITH, LIKE BELONGING, VALIDATION, AND MEANING.

The combination of people living longer and the pressure on one partner to meet all our needs resulted in the high rates of relationship breakdown and living alone that we have today. Many have questioned whether it's even possible to sustain companionship and passion over time, especially under the pressures that come with the nuclear family, of co-parenting and caring in relative isolation.

SCHOLAR & AUTHOR OF LOVE: A HISTORY, SIMON MAY

THE MONOGAMY/ NON-MONOGAMY BINARY

Mononormativity is **ethnocentric**. Globally, far more societies operate on some form of non-monogamy than monogamy. Many also form relationships on the basis of other things than romantic love and/or sexual attraction (e.g. money, work, family), and have different relationships to meet different needs (e.g. sex and companionship).

The rules of Western monogamy are pretty unclear and shift over time. People frequently only realize they follow different rules from one another once these have been broken, for example around flirting, kissing, solo sex, online porn or cybersex, close friendships, or friendships with ex-partners.

I COINED THE TERM "MONOGAMISH" TO RECOGNIZE THAT A LOT OF RELATIONSHIPS FALL SOMEWHERE BETWEEN MONOGAMY AND NON-MONOGAMY.

SEX ADVISOR & AUTHOR OF *SAVAGE LOVE*, DAN SAVAGE

Perhaps rather than a binary – with its problematic West vs rest and normal vs abnormal connotations – we should see monogamy and non-monogamy on a couple of spectrums. This would also recognize that people can be in different places in relation to romantic and erotic relationships.

SPECTRUM OF EMOTIONAL CLOSENESS

Monoamorous
ONE EMOTIONALLY CLOSE RELATIONSHIP, NO CLOSE RELATIONSHIPS BEYOND THIS

. . . .

Polyamorous
MULTIPLE EMOTIONALLY CLOSE RELATIONSHIPS

SPECTRUM OF PHYSICAL/ SEXUAL CONTACT

Monosexual
ONE SEXUAL RELATIONSHIP, NO SEX/ PHYSICAL CONTACT BEYOND THIS

. . . .

Polysexual
MULTIPLE, SEXUAL RELATIONSHIPS

ENDURING LOVE

Sociologist Jacqui Gabb found that those who do endure love often do so because they find ways to retain separateness as well as togetherness, helping them retain active appreciation for each other and nurture systems that support them and their relationship.

The existential philosophers pointed out that a key tension in relationships of all kinds is that between freedom and belonging. Given that romantic/erotic partnerships are now based on love and choice, this tension looms large there in particular.

LIVING APART TOGETHER

LIVING TOGETHER APART

These tensions can lead both to people treating relationships as disposable and to people staying too long in damaging relationships. In addition, the current exploration of diverse relationship styles could be seen as a response to this existential tension, and the primacy it has in current neoliberal culture.

NEW RELATIONSHIP *energy*

ROTA

> PEOPLE DESPAIR AT BEING ABANDONED TO THEIR OWN WITS, FEEL EASILY DISPOSABLE, AND YEARN FOR THE SECURITY OF TOGETHERNESS. THEY'RE DESPERATE TO RELATE. YET THEY'RE ALSO WARY OF "BEING RELATED", FEARING IT MAY BRING BURDENS AND STRAINS THEY AREN'T ABLE OR WILLING TO BEAR, AND MAY LIMIT THE FREEDOM THEY NEED IN ORDER TO RELATE!

SOCIOLOGIST & AUTHOR OF *LIQUID LOVE*, ZYGMUNT BAUMAN

DATING AND HOOK-UPS

The emphasis on love *and* choice means serial monogamy has become the most visible Western way of doing relationships. Dating is the accepted prequel to coupledom, and has become big business with online apps. Many are sold on the promise of finding the perfect love match, although people also use the apps to find friends and/or hook-up partners.

Feminist psychologists Pantea Farvid and Virginia Braun found people who had "casual sex" still saw this as inferior to monogamous relationships, requiring labour to avoid emotional engagement. There was no sense that hooking up with strangers, or having fuckbuddy arrangements with friends, could include emotion or be legitimate forms of intimacy.

STRAIGHT HOOK-UP CULTURE HAS IGNITED CONSERVATIVE CONCERNS ABOUT PROMISCUITY AND FEMINIST CRITIQUE OF HOW THE GAMIFICATION OF DATING APPS DISADVANTAGES WOMEN.

GENDER SCHOLAR & AUTHOR OF YES MEANS YES, **KATH ALBURY**

SORRY I DIDN'T GET BACK TO YOU. I'VE BEEN REALLY BUSY.

PING

NO WORRIES YOU'RE NOT ALL THAT ANYWAY LOL

PING

HOOK-UP APPS ARE AN IMPORTANT SITE OF SELF-REPRESENTATION WHERE GAY MEN CAN COMMUNICATE WHAT THEY VALUE ABOUT THEMSELVES. TAKING BACK THE MEANS OF PRODUCTION IS A POLITICAL ACT. BUT THEY ALSO REPLICATE THE STEREOTYPING AND DISCRIMINATION OF MAINSTREAM MEDIA

MEDIA SCHOLAR & AUTHOR OF GAYDAR CULTURE, **SHARIF MOWLABOCUS**

SORRY - NO FATS NO FEMMES NO ASIANS

BEAR LOOKING FOR ♥!

SECRET AND OPEN NON-MONOGAMIES

Mononormativity obscures the reality that most people are non-monogamous at some point. Rates of infidelity in Western culture are as high as 50–60%. Rather than exploring ways in which non-monogamy could be done more ethically, infidelity is still represented as scandalous, shameful, and dangerous.

PEOPLE STILL THINK LIFELONG MONOGAMY IS BEST FOR HAPPINESS, WELL-BEING, SEX, AND HAVING CHILDREN, DESPITE THE 5% OF THE POPULATION WHO ARE OPENLY NON-MONOGAMOUS BEING NO LESS SATISFIED WITH THEIR RELATIONSHIPS.

PSYCHOLOGIST TERRI CONLEY

There are many different styles of open consensual non-monogamies. These expand the possibilities for both emotional and erotic experiences or connections with multiple people.

MY RESEARCH FOUND THAT THE EXTRA EMOTIONAL AND PRACTICAL SUPPORT OF MULTIPLE ADULTS CAN ACTUALLY BE GREAT FOR CHILD-REARING.

RESEARCHER & AUTHOR OF THE POLYAMORISTS NEXT DOOR, ELISABETH SHEFF

IDEALISED MONOAMORY

CHEATING

"DON'T ASK, DON'T TELL"

OPEN RELATIONSHIP

POLYGAMY

POLY-FIDELITY

HIERARCHICAL POLYAMORY

EGALITARIAN POLYAMORY

SOLO POLYAMORY

RELATIONSHIP ANARCHY

POLYAMORY RULES

Consensually non-monogamous people put various rules and agreements in place to manage their relationships. Many open relationship styles draw a separation between love and sex: sex is allowed outside the primary partnership; love isn't.

BECAUSE POLYAMORY IS ABOUT EMOTIONAL – NOT JUST SEXUAL, CONNECTIONS – THERE ARE OFTEN RULES AROUND TIME, SPACE, AND CLOSENESS. LIKE ONLY PRIMARY PARTNERS COHABIT, OR CERTAIN EROTIC OR EVERYDAY ACTIVITIES ARE KEPT SACRED FOR SPECIFIC RELATIONSHIPS.

SOCIOLOGIST **KASSIA WOSICK-CORREA**

Polyamorous people differ on how much they disclose about other partners, and whether they prefer clear agreements or flexibility to allow each relationship to develop.

Polyamory can teach us a lot about open communication, intentional relationships, and developing languages to recognize different kinds of relationship and emotional experience (such as "metamour" for a partner's partner, and "compersion" for a positive opposite of jealousy). However, it can carry the risk of objectifying partners classified as "secondary" or otherwise lesser.

A RISK OF INFATUATION WITH THIS IDEA OF NOT CHOOSING IS THAT, SINCE ANYTHING IS POSSIBLE, THEN EVERYTHING MUST BE DONE. THIS CAN INTERFERE WITH HAVING ENOUGH TIME AND ENERGY FOR RELATIONSHIPS AND OTHER ASPECTS OF LIFE.

SOCIOLOGIST **DANIEL CARDOSO**

POLYNORMATIVITY

As with hook-up culture, there's a tendency for consensual non-monogamies to reproduce many aspects of mononormativity, even as they question the idea that it's possible to have sex with – or to love – more than one person. Sex educator and blogger Andrea Zanin (aka Sex Geek) came up with the following elements of polynormativity:

- Polyamory starts with a couple.
- Polyamory is hierarchical.
- Polyamory requires a lot of rules.
- Polyamory is heterosexual-ish, cute, young, and white.

The search for The One true partner might be replaced by the search for the Poly Grail of the perfect set of partners. The sense that romantic partnerships are more important than other relationships often remains – as does pressure to be sexual within them.

DESPITE DESCRIBING MANAGING THEIR RELATIONSHIPS IN QUITE SIMILAR WAYS, POLYGAMOUS IMMIGRANTS ARE TREATED FAR MORE NEGATIVELY THAN WHITE POLYAMORISTS LEGALLY AND IN THE MEDIA.

SEXUALITY SCHOLAR & AUTHOR OF FRAUGHT INTIMACIES, NATHAN RAMBUKKANA

EXCLUSION AND FETISHIZATION OF BLACK PEOPLE ARE BOTH REAL PROBLEMS IN POLYAMOROUS COMMUNITIES.

ACTIVIST & AUTHOR OF LOVE'S NOT COLORBLIND, KEVIN PATTERSON

AROMANTIC EXPERIENCE

Aromantic – or aro – experience radically troubles the emphasis our culture puts on romantic love, given aromantic people don't experience it. Bringing asexual and aromantic experience together, we can see that it's perfectly possible to feel romantic attraction without sexual, sexual attraction without romantic, or neither. This resonates with current scientific understanding (see pp.49 and 65). We might all usefully locate ourselves – and different relationships in our lives – on the following spectrums, noticing whether our position shifts over time.

ASEXUAL <--------> HIGH SEXUAL ATTRACTION
AROMANTIC <--------> HIGH ROMANTIC ATTRACTION

And we might consider the different kinds of attraction we do or do not experience in different relationships.

ROMANTIC ♥ ATTRACTION

SEXUAL ATTRACTION

♥Crushes♥

SENSUAL (not sexual) ATTRACTION (tactile sensations like cuddles)

SQUISHES (platonic crushes)

AESTHETIC attraction (no desire to do anything sexual or romantic – just appreciating appearance)

This also helps us to think about consent in relation to much more than sex. Just as the sexual imperative pressures people to be sexual in a certain way, so mononormativity pressures people to experience particular emotional experiences in relationships and to make certain commitments. Aro experience encourages us to view platonic relationships, friends-with-benefits arrangements, and other relationship forms as equally valid as romantic partnerships.

RELATIONSHIP ANARCHY, DECOLONIAL LOVE, AND ACCESS INTIMACY

Relationship anarchy (RA) challenges hierarchies between romantic/sexual relationships and other kinds, arguing that relationships shouldn't be bound by rules other than those mutually agreed by the people in them.

The related idea of decolonial love locates current mononormativity in the histories of colonialism, slavery, and capitalism, which involved treating other people as things for personal gain. As author and activist Philippe Leonard Fradet notes, decolonial love involves ongoing critical reflection on power dynamics and consent. It commits to never treating another person – or yourself – as property which somebody is entitled to, or from whom certain forms of labour are expected. A related concept from disability activism is access intimacy.

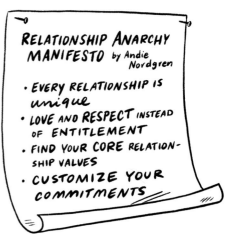

RELATIONSHIP ANARCHY MANIFESTO by Andie Nordgren

- EVERY RELATIONSHIP IS unique
- LOVE AND RESPECT INSTEAD OF ENTITLEMENT
- FIND YOUR CORE RELATIONSHIP VALUES
- CUSTOMIZE YOUR COMMITMENTS

These ideas remind us that we're interconnected with other species and the ecosystem as well as other humans.

SEX WORK

Sex workers remain one of the most stigmatized, pathologized, and criminalized groups within the arena of sexuality. Whorephobia often goes unquestioned where other prejudices would be challenged. Public discourse frequently denies sex workers any agency over their lives and presents them as morally suspect and polluting. Legislation puts sex workers at great risk by forcing them to operate under dangerous conditions in order to practice legally or avoid arrest.

MEDIA REPRESENTATIONS SUGGEST THAT SEX WORKERS ARE ONLY HAPPY "HIGH CLASS" CALL GIRLS OR TRAFFICKED WOMEN VICTIMS. THE VAST MAJORITY DON'T FIT EITHER CATEGORY. WHEN SEX WORKERS SPEAK OF THEIR MOTIVATIONS, THEY TALK ABOUT THE NEED TO EARN A LIVABLE INCOME – WITH MOTHERHOOD, DISABILITY, MIGRANCY, RACE, CARING RESPONSIBILITIES, AND TRANS EXPERIENCE SHAPING THESE REALITIES.

SEX WORKER ACTIVISTS & AUTHORS OF REVOLTING PROSTITUTES, MOLLY SMITH & JUNO MAC

I NEED YOU TO STAY HERE FOR AN HOUR, OKAY? MUMMY NEEDS TO WORK.

In many situations sex work is the most viable – or only – option in a world where, for example, mothers are expected to work in the home unpaid and there is little financial support available to disabled people.

SEX WORK AND SEX

Like aromantic people and relationship anarchists, sex workers challenge mononormativity because they engage in sexual encounters with multiple people and for reasons other than romantic love. Like asexual people, they also trouble the sexual imperative by having sex for reasons other than sexual attraction.

By questioning these binaries, sex worker activists remind us of the uncomfortable truths that:

PERHAPS SOME OF THE REASONS FOR THE STIGMATIZATION OF SEX WORK ARE THE DESIRE TO MAINTAIN – OFTEN CLASSED AND RACED – BINARIES BETWEEN GOOD WOMEN AND BAD WHORES, AND BETWEEN FREE AGENTIC WOMEN AND VICTIM PROSTITUTES WHO ARE IN NEED OF SAVING.

MOLLY SMITH & JUNO MAC

- People often have sex for implicit or explicit exchange (e.g. for gifts, dates, housework, romance, validation, peace).

I BETTER GET LAID FOR THIS

COME ON, BABY. DIDN'T WE HAVE A GOOD TIME TONIGHT?

- Sex is increasingly experienced as a form of labour for all of us - particularly women - under neoliberal capitalism (see p.90).

DO I EEP TRYING R JUST FAKE IT NOW?

- Under conditions of social injustice, power imbalances, and limited sexual scripts, the amount of sexual agency that anyone - particularly women - has is questionable.

SEX WORK AND WORK

Stigmatizing sex workers as bad versus other types of workers as good obscures the unjust capitalist culture which means that many people have to work long hours for low pay in precarious jobs that they hate, while other – more privileged people – benefit from their labour and get to enjoy their work.

IT CAN BE USEFUL TO QUESTION THE BOUNDARIES BETWEEN "LEGITIMATE" OCCUPATIONS THAT INVOLVE PHYSICAL TOUCH AND/OR EMOTIONAL LABOUR – LIKE THERAPIST, MASSEUR, SPORTS COACH – AND FORMS OF SEX WORK.

SEXUALITY SCHOLAR ALLAN TYLER

Suspicion around sex work obscures the fact that most types of workers have to engage in emotional labour – feigning enjoyment to clients and managers.

As we saw in the last chapter, focusing on transgression rather than coercion causes problems. Instead of working to police all forms of transgressive sex (including sex work), we could work to prevent all forms of coercive work: human trafficking, forced labour, and exploitation (including sexual exploitation). However, this may well involve facing difficult questions about reparations for historical slavery, the way we all benefit from cheap labour, and the exploitation and harassment involved in everyday workplaces.

SINGLEDOM AND SOLO RELATIONSHIPS

For some people, the primary relationship is the nurturing and/or erotic one they have with themselves.

YOU NEED TO FIND THE ONE.

I ALREADY HAVE, THANK YOU. I'M SELF-PARTNERED.

ACTOR & ACTIVIST EMMA WATSON

DON'T WORRY, YOU'LL GET A PARTNER SOON.

I HAVE SEVERAL PARTNERS, BUT MY PRIMARY RELATIONSHIP IS WITH MYSELF: I'M SINGLEISH.

AUTHOR OF RADICAL RELATING, MEL CASSIDY

DON'T YOU NEED SOMEONE TO COMPLETE YOU?

SOLO POLY PEOPLE LIKE ME REFUSE THE RELATIONSHIP ESCALATOR TOWARDS MERGED LIVES AND IDENTITIES.

AUTHOR OF STEPPING OFF THE RELATIONSHIP ESCALATOR, AMY GAHRAN

Solo relationships are stigmatized as relationship styles, with cultural assumptions that people must want romantic partnership. **Couple privilege** refers to the many legal and practical benefits afforded to couples, as well as the expectation by many that romantic partners come first before other relationships in their lives.

The term **incel** (involuntary celibate) captures those excluded from erotic and/or romantic relationships due to norms of attraction, marginalization, and/or neurodiversity – raising awareness that not all people have the same access to couple privilege and sex with others. However, as media professor Debbie Ging points out, the term was appropriated by straight white men who felt entitled to sex from women and victimized by systems that privilege certain forms of masculinity.

SOLO SEX

So far, we've mostly considered relationship contexts for sex which involve another person or people. However, much – if not most – of the sex people have is with themselves.

Solo sex is possible within all relationship styles, with the exception of forms of monogamy which are so tight they exclude it as a form of infidelity. However, there's often stigma around it and preference for partnered sex.

SOLO SEX IS STILL SEEN AS INFERIOR TO SEX WITH OTHERS: SELF-INDULGENT, PART OF A PHASE ON THE WAY TO BEING A "PROPER" SEXUAL BEING, AND/OR AS SOMETHING THAT WE COULD DO AS "PRACTICE" FOR THE "REAL THING". IF WE DO ENJOY IT, IT'S REGARDED AS RISKY, POTENTIALLY ADDICTIVE.

COMMUNICATION SCHOLAR & AUTO(EROTIC)ETHNOGRAPHER KRISTEN C. BLINNE

We can expand the concept of solo sex to include all forms of erotic activity with ourselves.

SOLO AND/OR SHARED?

Susanna Paasonen, author of *Many Splendored Things*, points out that people sharing fantasies, amateur porn, and webcam sessions online blurs boundaries between sex and play, and solo and other sex.

One common type of online erotica involves fans "slashing" or "shipping" fictional characters from their favourite TV programmes, books, and movies. This challenges assumptions about:

- Gender and sexuality, as it's often written by straight women about male-male couples
- The default sexual script, as it incorporates diverse practices
- The appropriate relationship context for sex, as platonic friends get turned on by each other's writing
- The need to be in the same place - or even time - as each other for an erotic exchange, as people often write and read out of sync with one another.

As with all forms of sex, writing/reading erotica means different things for different people at different times. It can be fun, intellectually stimulating, hot, healing, and more.

RETURNING TO NORMAL

So far, we've seen how sexuality has been delineated according to a normal/abnormal binary, in terms of people's identities based on attraction, activities, desires and relationships

We've uncovered a moral binary interwoven with this which presumes a normal majority – of heterosexual monogamous couples having PIV sex – and an abnormal minority. But when we add up all the people who have other erotic attractions, bodily experiences, sexual desires, and relationships, they form the vast majority, not the minority.

So, in addition to moving away from a normal/abnormal binary, we can challenge minority/majority models. Shifting away from this helps us to see diversity, rather than a binary, and to consider what we all might learn from people with different ideas and practices than our own.

CHAPTER 6: HOW SEX WORKS

How do we come to have an inner sense of our own sexuality? And how does it develop in the ways it does over time? These questions have generally been framed to search for explanations for those outside the supposed "norm".

Sexualities outside the norm are regarded as requiring evidence and explanation or called into question entirely.

Philosopher Talia Mae Bettcher argues that this basic denial of authenticity denies marginalized people first-person authority over their own sexualities and genders.

Along with normal/abnormal, another binary haunts these questions of cause or explanation. The nature/nurture binary assumes that the reason somebody is a "sexual minority", "sexually dysfunctional", or "paraphilic" must be down to either biology or experience: Were they born that way or made that way? Is it innate or did it develop?

NATURE OR NURTURE?

NATURE VS NURTURE HAS DOGGED SEXOLOGY OVER TIME, WITH THE ANSWERS SHIFTING RADICALLY. MOST EARLY SEXOLOGISTS ASSUMED SEXUAL "DEVIANCE" TO BE A PHYSICAL ILLNESS (NATURE) WHEREAS FREUD'S THEORY LOCATED IT IN CHILDHOOD STAGES (NURTURE).

WHEN MASTERS AND JOHNSON DID THEIR RESEARCH, SEXUAL PROBLEMS WERE BELIEVED TO BE 90% PSYCHOLOGICAL, WHEREAS IN THESE DAYS OF BIG PHARMA THE ESTIMATE IS 80% PHYSIOLOGICAL.

SOCIOLOGIST & AUTHOR OF *SEXUAL* VÉRONIQUE MOTTIER

SEX THERAPIST
PEGGY KLEINPLATZ

Some who support the search for causation argue that it's important because if we can prove a biological cause for some aspect of sexuality it'll be more accepted. However, Eve Kosofsky Sedgwick points out that whatever the prevailing scientific opinion on homosexuality, it has always been seen as deficient (e.g. overprotective mothers – nurture, or feminized brains – nature).

NATURE vs NURTURE

OUR RESEARCH FOUND THAT THERE'S LITTLE EVIDENCE THAT PROMOTING BIOLOGICAL UNDERSTANDINGS MAKES PEOPLE LESS HOMOPHOBIC.

SOCIAL PSYCHOLOGISTS PETER HEGARTY & FELICIA PRATTO

NATURAL ASSUMPTIONS

Scientists searching for biological explanations have often come from the biased starting point that procreative sex is the most natural kind, drawing on the animal world to justify this claim. However, biologist Joan Roughgarden and sociologist Myra Hird point out animal species have sex for many other reasons than procreation, for example:

- Sex can strengthen bonds between animals or groups.
- Many animals masturbate.
- Many have oral sex, anal sex, and use forms of birth control.
- Trans-species sex can't result in procreation.
- Same-sex sex happens in more than half of mammal and bird species, sometimes more often than hetero sex.
- Very few species are monogamous or pair-bond for life.

NATURE, THEN, IS NEITHER STATIC NOR OBVIOUS.

BIOLOGIST & AUTHOR OF SEX/GENDER, ANNE FAUSTO-STERLING

NATURALNESS CONNOTES NO INTRINSIC MORAL VALUE AT ALL, AND NORMAL IS ONLY A NUMBER.

JESSE BERING

"Natural" and "normal" are often conflated, with arguments to nature only generally being deployed to support normative assumptions about sex. The question of causation assumes that we can draw these normal/abnormal distinctions and that there could be one universal reason for being in the "abnormal" category, rather than many different pathways that lead someone to their attractions, desires, and practices.

BIOPSYCHOSOCIAL

Sexuality is always biopsychosocial. Our body and brain ("bio") influence – and are influenced by – our individual experience ("psycho") and our wider culture and the messages we receive ("social"). These continue to influence one another over our lifetime. We could never disentangle these aspects of a person's sexuality.

Let's look at some examples of how each of these things influences the others.

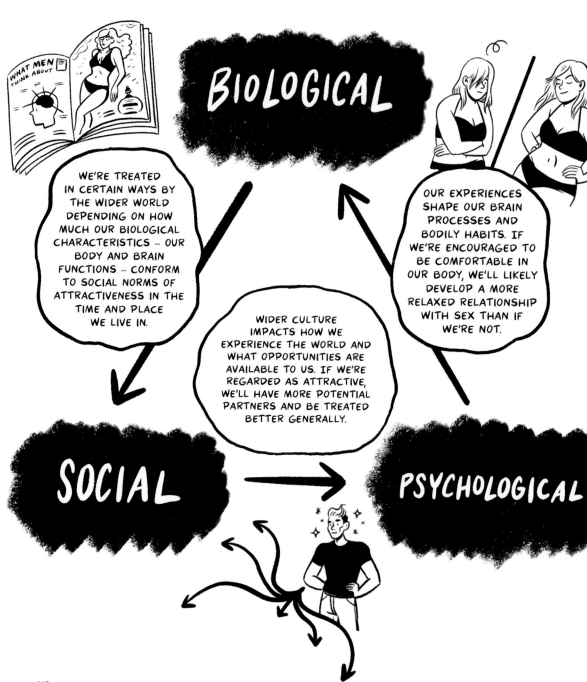

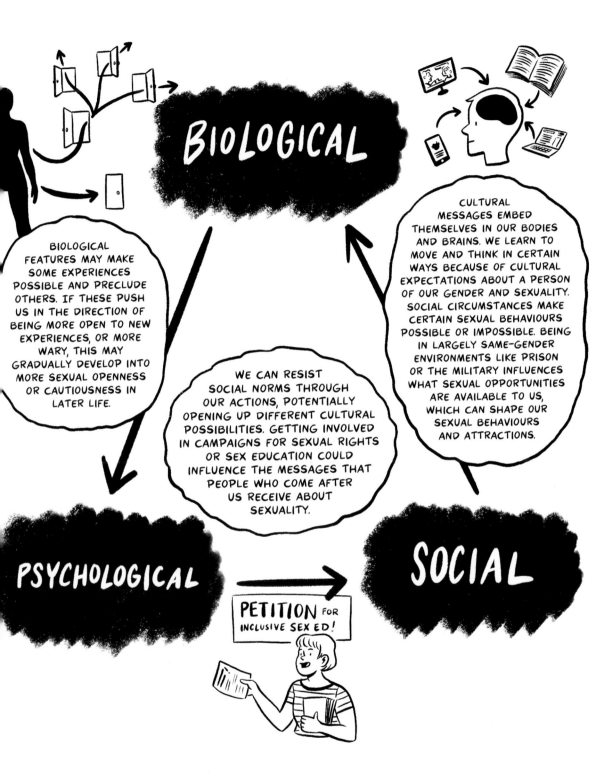

BIOLOGICAL

BIOLOGICAL FEATURES MAY MAKE SOME EXPERIENCES POSSIBLE AND PRECLUDE OTHERS. IF THESE PUSH US IN THE DIRECTION OF BEING MORE OPEN TO NEW EXPERIENCES, OR MORE WARY, THIS MAY GRADUALLY DEVELOP INTO MORE SEXUAL OPENNESS OR CAUTIOUSNESS IN LATER LIFE.

WE CAN RESIST SOCIAL NORMS THROUGH OUR ACTIONS, POTENTIALLY OPENING UP DIFFERENT CULTURAL POSSIBILITIES. GETTING INVOLVED IN CAMPAIGNS FOR SEXUAL RIGHTS OR SEX EDUCATION COULD INFLUENCE THE MESSAGES THAT PEOPLE WHO COME AFTER US RECEIVE ABOUT SEXUALITY.

CULTURAL MESSAGES EMBED THEMSELVES IN OUR BODIES AND BRAINS. WE LEARN TO MOVE AND THINK IN CERTAIN WAYS BECAUSE OF CULTURAL EXPECTATIONS ABOUT A PERSON OF OUR GENDER AND SEXUALITY. SOCIAL CIRCUMSTANCES MAKE CERTAIN SEXUAL BEHAVIOURS POSSIBLE OR IMPOSSIBLE. BEING IN LARGELY SAME-GENDER ENVIRONMENTS LIKE PRISON OR THE MILITARY INFLUENCES WHAT SEXUAL OPPORTUNITIES ARE AVAILABLE TO US, WHICH CAN SHAPE OUR SEXUAL BEHAVIOURS AND ATTRACTIONS.

PSYCHOLOGICAL

SOCIAL

PETITION FOR INCLUSIVE SEX ED!

We can't possibly tease apart which aspects of a person's sexuality are bio, psycho, or social. But even if we could, it shouldn't affect the way we treat people.

STRUCTURE AND AGENCY

People often assume that being biologically caused makes something more "real" than being the result of social norms and/or personal experience. If a sexuality isn't clearly biological, it's often regarded as a "lifestyle choice", with the sense that people could – and probably should – choose otherwise. The natural = real idea conflates a number of different binaries. We can't put any human experience on one side or the other of any of these:

- Nature (biological) vs nurture (social)
- Essential (a fixed aspect of our very essence) vs constructed (shaped by wider forces)
- Determined (caused by internal or external factors) vs free (chosen), also referred to as structure vs agency.

How free are we to determine how we experience and express our sexuality? How much is this determined by the structures around us?

SOCIETY'S CONCEPTION OF SEXUALITY INEVITABLY SHAPES OUR BEHAVIOUR AND OUR UNDERSTANDING OF OURSELVES AS SEXUAL BEINGS.

Our sexualities are shaped by cultural messages and social structures which determine how much freedom we have (around money, healthcare, travel, etc.). Less restrictive structures, and more diverse messages, give us more agency to choose, and vice versa.

AUTHOR OF *ALL YOU NEED TO KNOW... SEXUALITY*, CHARLIE McCANN

SIMON AND GAGNON: SEXUAL SCRIPTS

We've seen throughout this book that we're all exposed to a similar set of cultural messages and scripts around sexuality (heteronormativity, the sexual imperative, normal/abnormal and functional/dysfunctional binaries, etc.).

IN ANY GIVEN SOCIETY, AT ANY GIVEN MOMENT IN ITS HISTORY, PEOPLE BECOME SEXUAL IN THE SAME WAY THEY BECOME EVERYTHING ELSE. WITHOUT MUCH REFLECTION, THEY PICK UP DIRECTIONS FROM THEIR SOCIAL ENVIRONMENT. THEY ACQUIRE AND ASSEMBLE MEANINGS, SKILLS, AND VALUES FROM THE PEOPLE AROUND THEM.

How do our ways of experiencing, identifying, and expressing our sexualities end up so diverse? Simon and Gagnon's sexual script theory suggest a series of embedded influences. These include the scripts available to us in our particular wider culture, but also in the communities and institutions we're part of, in our interpersonal relationships now and the families and other groups we grew up in, and in our unique set of lived experiences plus the intrapsychic conversations we have with ourselves about them.

RESISTANCE OR REINFORCEMENT?

At each level, messages about sexuality might be reinforced, or resisted. We might be presented with limited options, or a wider range of possibilities, which can expand or contract our sense of agency. These things will shift over time too as our culture, communities, relationships, and experience of ourselves change.

GROWING UP, WIDER CULTURE GAVE ME A HETERONORMATIVE SEXUAL SCRIPT, WHICH MY SCHOOL AND FAMILY REINFORCED.

WOMYN FEST

BUT I FOUND LESBIAN COMMUNITIES WHICH RESISTED THIS AND HELPED ME FIND A DIFFERENT SCRIPT AND MY RELATIONSHIPS WITH WOMEN HELPED ME TO FIND MY IDENTITY AND EXPRESSION.

BUT NOW ...

I KEEP GETTING THE MESSAGE THAT RELATIONSHIPS MUST BE SEXUAL. MY COMMUNITY AND FRIENDS ALSO TELL ME THAT I SHOULD BE WITH A WOMAN TO BE A "PROPER LESBIAN". IT'S HARD TO RECONCILE THIS WITH HOW I FEEL AND WHAT I WANT TO DO NOW. MAYBE I NEED TO JOIN NEW COMMUNITIES AND RELATIONSHIPS TO SUPPORT THIS CHANGE.

KEN PLUMMER: SEXUAL STORIES

Sociologist Ken Plummer developed sexual script theory in his theory of sexual stories.

> WE ALL TELL NARRATIVES ABOUT WHO WE ARE AND HOW WE CAME TO BE THAT WAY. WE REPEAT THESE TO OURSELVES AND TO OTHERS TO MAKE SENSE OF OUR LIVES AND TO PRESENT OURSELVES IN CERTAIN WAYS. THESE OFTEN DRAW ON THE STORIES CIRCULATING IN THE MEDIA AND THE COMMUNITIES WE INHABIT.

Today sex has become the big story, with people telling tales of their sexuality in talk shows, magazines, over social media, to therapists, in support groups, and to friends. This means stories often take on similar structures and contain the same key elements. For example:

Stories are joint actions. They require the storytellers who produce accounts; the coaxers, coaches, and coercers who have the power to elicit stories from the tellers; and the consumers of the story. The stories that consumers engage with influence the stories that they themselves tell.

#METOO AND SEXUAL STORIES

#MeToo is a recent sexual story.

> HEARING THESE STORIES ENABLED MANY TO RECOGNIZE THEMSELVES AS SURVIVORS WITHIN A CULTURE WHICH OFTEN MINIMIZES SEXUAL VIOLENCE AND BLAMES VICTIMS. IT EXPOSED OFTEN POWERFUL WHITE MALE PERPETRATORS AND HIGHLIGHTED SEXUAL VIOLENCE AS A STRUCTURAL PROBLEM, LIFTING THE SENSE OF RESPONSIBILITY FROM INDIVIDUAL SURVIVORS.

AUTHOR OF *DIGITAL FEMINIST ACTIVISM*, **KAITLYNN MENDES**

> SEXUAL VIOLENCE KNOWS NO RACE, CLASS OR GENDER, BUT THE RESPONSE TO IT DOES.

However, certain stories receiving prominence inevitably leads to some people being more able to see themselves reflected and share their stories than others. Experiences of women of colour were often sidelined, despite #MeToo having originated in their communities.

ORIGINATOR OF #METOO, TARANA BURKE

> MAINSTREAM FEMINISM CENTRES PRIVILEGED WHITE WOMEN AS VICTIMS AND DEMANDS THAT 'BAD MEN' BE PUNISHED, BOLSTERING THE CRIMINAL JUSTICE SYSTEM WHICH HARMS MARGINALIZED PEOPLE.

AUTHOR OF *ME NOT YOU*, ALISON PHIPPS

#MeToo can reinforce existing hierarchies of more or less legitimate kinds of survivors and/or abuse, as well as focusing attention on specific individuals rather than the systems that support them. However some systemic change has resulted from #MeToo, with many companies revising their harassment policies, for example (more in Chapter 7).

MEDIATED INTIMACY AND SEXUAL SUBJECTIFICATION

WE NOW LIVE IN A WORLD SUFFUSED AND SATURATED WITH REPRESENTATIONS OF INTIMATE RELATIONSHIPS, BOTH IN THE MEDIA WE BUY AND THE MEDIA WE PRODUCE OURSELVES. MEDIA FROM ROMCOMS AND PORN, TO MEMOIRS AND SEX APPS, CONSTITUTE OUR PRIMARY SOURCE OF INFORMATION ABOUT WHAT INTIMACY LOOKS AND FEELS LIKE. IN THIS WAY INTIMACY IS ALWAYS MEDIATED.

ROS GILL

Neoliberal values drive people to present newer and better versions of themselves to the world, becoming entrepreneurs of the self. We internalize and replicate the stories we're sold of sexuality and selfhood which reinforce a sense of individual lack and failure.

This can mean we become hypervigilant self-monitors, curating outward images of successful sexual selves, while harshly judging and criticizing ourselves. These stories are a cultural gaslighting that obscures the real causes of our suffering and distracts us from the problematic systems and structures actually responsible.

DOING ORGASMS

A good example of mediated intimacy is orgasm. On page 68 we mentioned how the pressure on women to provide a - real or fake - orgasm to reassure (male) partners is a kind of female emotional labour.

THIS CONFORMS TO THE GENERAL EXPECTATION THAT WOMEN WILL FEED EGOS AND TEND WOUNDS.

PHILOSOPHER & AUTHOR OF *FEMININITY AND DOMINATION*, SANDRA BARTKY

DUDE, WE TOTALLY HIT THIRD BASE!

I BET SHE DIDN'T EVEN CUM

Because women's orgasms aren't deemed self-evident, women are required to demonstrate a spectacular performance. Women have a felt need to show appreciation for male sexual performance whether or not they really experience orgasm, so similar performances accompany "real" and "fake" orgasms.

WE LEARN WHAT SEXUAL AROUSAL LOOKS AND SOUNDS LIKE FROM THE MOVIES, AND - AS WITH ANY OTHER LANGUAGE - WE PICK UP THE GRAMMAR AND SYNTAX WITHOUT BEING AWARE OF IT.

CULTURAL THEORIST & AUTHOR OF *UNBEARABLE WEIGHT*, SUSAN BORDO

Sociologists and authors of *Theorizing Sexuality*, Stevi Jackson and Sue Scott point out that we learn to "do" orgasm in an embodied way, drawing on media representations to make sense of our own sensations and to communicate desire and pleasure to others.

WHEN HARRY MET SALLY FAKE ORGASM SCENE

INTERSECTIONAL SEXUALITY

We've talked about "the media" and "culture", but of course not everyone internalizes the same messages about sexuality.

We have diverse sexualities partly because of the erotic options available to us or not – at our specific intersectional location – which also change over time. Oppression and marginalization can limit our agency and erotic possibilities.

However, critical race and queer theorists highlight how migrant and mixed race people challenge fixed identities and normal/abnormal, minority/majority binaries, offering ways we might all shift away from unidimensional understandings of sexuality.

IMMIGRATION IS CONTINUALLY CONSTRUCTED AS A "CRISIS" AND PEOPLE OF COLOUR'S SEXUALITY, RELATIONSHIPS, AND FAMILY STRUCTURES POSITIONED AS PATHOLOGICAL AND A THREAT TO "TRADITIONAL VALUES" AND AUTHORITY RELATIONS.

CRITICAL PSYCHOLOGIST & AUTHOR OF RACE, GENDER, SOCIAL WELFARE, GAIL LEWIS

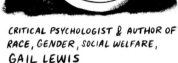

LIVING ON THE BORDERLANDS HELPS US SEE THE ARBITRARY NATURE OF ALL SOCIAL CATEGORIES, AND HOW OPPRESSIONS ARE FLUID SYSTEMS THAT TAKE ON DIFFERENT FORMS AND NUANCES IN DIFFERENT CONTEXTS.

QUEER THEORIST
GLORIA ANZALDUA

QUEERS OF COLOUR ARE NOT COMFORTABLY SITUATED IN ANY ONE DISCOURSE OF MINORITY SUBJECTIVITY. HYBRID IDENTIFICATORY POSITIONS ARE ALWAYS IN TRANSIT.

QUEER THEORIST & AUTHOR OF CRUISING UTOPIA, JOSÉ ESTEBAN MUÑOZ

IDENTITY OR FLUIDITY?

As Anzaldúa and Muñoz suggest, our sexualities are fluid and ever unfolding: a set of stories that we tell to make sense of our experiences, in dialogue with our wider culture, communities, and the people around us with whom we have erotic encounters and talk about sex.

DESIRE — AND THUS DESIRING SUBJECTS — CANNOT BE PLACED INTO DISCRETE IDENTITY CATEGORIES WHICH REMAIN STATIC FOR THE DURATION OF PEOPLE'S LIVES.

PSYCHOANALYTIC PSYCHOTHERAPIST & PSYCHOSOCIAL THEORIST, NOREEN GIFFNEY

Queer approaches are therefore critical of "identity politics" which fight for sexual rights on the basis of being a certain kind of person, often with a sense that those outside normativity have to come out and confess or explain their sexualities in order to justify receiving rights or acceptance.

IDENTITY SHOULD BE A SPACE TO NEGOTIATE SOCIAL CONTRADICTIONS, RATHER THAN A SPACE WHERE DIFFERENCES ARE CONCEALED FOR THE SAKE OF STABILITY.

SEXUALITY SCHOLAR & CREATOR OF QUEER OF COLOR CRITIQUE, RODERICK FERGUSON

ATTRACTION
DESIRES
ACTIVITIES
SEXUALITY
RELATIONS
ENCOUNTERS

LET'S DO THE TIME WARP!

HOW CAN WE MAKE SENSE OF OUR EROTIC EXPERIENCES WITHOUT FINDING OURSELVES BACK IN ATTEMPTS TO EXPLAIN THE CAUSES AND ESSENTIALIZE OURSELVES?

PSYCHOLOGIST & AUTHOR OF SEXUALITY: A PSYCHOSOCIAL MANIFESTO, KATHERINE JOHNSON

EROTIC ASSEMBLAGES

One way to make sense of sexual experience without essentializing us is assemblage theory. This sees us – as human bodies – as only part of the whole "assemblage" of any sexual experience. Academics and authors of *Sociology and the New Materialism*, Pam Alldred and Nick Fox illustrate this with an example of a kiss. If we're just thinking about the humans involved we might imagine that the kissing assemblage is this:

However, seeing the human as only part of the picture we can recognize that there's a whole lot more to the kissing assemblage. All of these elements can enable or block the ways in which desire – and other emotional or bodily experiences – can flow through us.

So we can problematize the idea that "a kiss is just a kiss", something mechanical and straightforward that means the same thing for everyone. The same is true for any aspect of sexuality.

EROTIC FANTASY

Where does all this leave us with the common idea – since Freud – that our sexual desires reveal important truths about ourselves: the kind of people that we are? While we can question any universal theories explaining specific desires or attractions, there is potentially a great deal of self-understanding to be gained from tuning into our sexual desires and fantasies.

Fantasy can be as simple as picturing a certain person or act when you're turned on, or as complex as a detailed movie or story in your mind. We can feed and develop them by seeking out images, videos, or stories created by others which depict similar fantasies; by imagining, writing, or drawing them ourselves; or by acting them out alone or with others.

BARBARELLA

MY SECRET GARDEN
WOMEN'S SEXUAL FANTASIES
NANCY FRIDAY

Garden of Desires
The Evolution of WOMEN'S SEXUAL FANTASIES
Emily Dubberley

MOST AMERICANS HAVE SEXUAL FANTASIES ABOUT GROUP SEX, BONDAGE, DOMINATION, SUBMISSION, FORCED SEX, OPEN RELATIONSHIPS, AND SEX TOYS. TUNING INTO OUR DESIRES – AND SHARING THEM – CAN DISPEL THE MYTHS AROUND WHAT IS AND ISN'T NORMAL AND HELP US ALL TOWARDS BETTER SEX.

SENSE 8

PSYCHOLOGIST & AUTHOR OF TELL ME WHAT YOU WANT, JUSTIN LEHMILLER

Tuning into our fantasies to learn what turns us on can be seen as pretty radical in the face of the restrictive sexual norms that we've covered in this book.

LEARNING FROM FANTASY

While there's a lot of common content across people's fantasies, there are no universal explanations for what they mean. Rather, like dreams, they have specific meanings when we understand that person's life.

OUR CORE EROTIC THEMES CAN OFTEN DEVELOP OUT OF THE TOUGH TIMES OF OUR LIVES WHICH ARE, OF COURSE, DIFFERENT FOR EACH OF US. WE MAY USE SEXUAL FANTASIES TO TRANSFORM EMOTIONALLY DIFFICULT EXPERIENCES INTO SOMETHING PLEASURABLE. IT'S A SMART SURVIVAL STRATEGY.

AUTHOR OF *THE EROTIC MIND*, JACK MORIN

I WAS BULLIED AT SCHOOL. IN MY FANTASIES I IMAGINE BEING TOUGH AND STRONG, EASILY DOMINATING POWERFUL PEOPLE LIKE MY BULLIES.

I WAS BULLIED TOO, BUT I LOVE HURT-COMFORT STORIES, WHERE I ENDURE SOMETHING TOUGH BUT THEN GET LOOKED AFTER. I GUESS I WISH THAT'D HAPPENED TO ME.

This helps us to understand why so many fantasies involve themes of difficult experiences like pain, power, non-consent, and shame.

Tuning into our fantasies can be personally helpful: revealing our key patterns and survival strategies, helping us towards greater self-understanding and self-compassion. This is a radical, political act within a culture which encourages us to self-monitor, self-criticize, and pretend to be "normal".

THE PERSONAL IS POLITICAL

Tuning into our fantasies can also help us to be more consensual with others.

THE MAIN DANGER WITH TURN-ONS WHICH DISTURB US ARISES WHEN WE TRY TO DENY THEM AND HIDE THEM FROM OURSELVES. WE MAY WELL END UP REPRESSING THEM AND/OR ACTING THEM OUT NON-CONSENSUALLY.

Turning towards fantasy with openness and curiosity can enable us to make ethical decisions about which to keep as fantasies, which we might act out with consenting partners, and which we might creatively engage with in other ways.

Our fantasies emerge within a particular social context as well as within the context of our own lived experiences. The popularity of fantasies of power play and forced sex make sense in such a non-consensual culture, as we'll explore in the next chapter.

FANTASY IS NEVER JUST ABOUT THE CONTENT OF THE FANTASY BUT ALSO ABOUT THE STRUCTURAL POSITION AND SOCIAL CONTEXT OF ITS WRITERS AND CONSUMERS.

SCI-FI AUTHOR & LITERARY CRITIC JOANNA RUSS

EXPANDING THE EROTIC

In Chapter 1 we saw how libertarians and revolutionaries viewed sexual liberation and cultural revolution as going hand in hand. Turning towards fantasy as simultaneously individual and social, personal and political, could realize such radical potentials.

> EROTICA CAN CREATE A SAFE IMAGINATIVE SPACE TO WORK THROUGH THE HORRORS OF OPPRESSION: COMING TO TERMS WITH COMPLEX ISSUES OF CONSENT, WILL, AGENCY, AND DESIRE.

GENDER SCHOLAR & AUTHOR OF STRIPPING, SEX, AND POPULAR CULTURE, CATHERINE M. ROACH

> FEAR, DESTRUCTION, HORNINESS, AND RELEASE ARE LAYERED ONTO EACH OTHER IN QUEER MEN'S SEXUALITY LIKE FLAKY PASTRY. THIS IS SIMULTANEOUSLY DEFIANT, AS WE HAVE EROTICIZED THAT WHICH HAS SOUGHT TO DESTROY US, AND TAINTED, AS IT CREATES A PRECARIOUSNESS AT THE HEART OF QUEER MEN'S EXPERIENCE.

SEX WORK ACTIVIST JACK SAUL

(Re)claiming the erotic is complex, but engaging with existing erotic stories – and creating our own in fantasy or play – can expand our erotic imaginations and the wider sexual stories out there.

WHAT DO YOU THINK OF THE POWER DYNAMICS IN THIS BIT?

GIRL ON THE NET

> EROTIC STORIES THAT ARE PERSONAL, EMBODIED, AND RELATIONAL PROVIDE ONE WITH AN OPPORTUNITY TO REVISIT AND RE-STORY ONE'S OWN JOURNEY BY REFLECTING, ASKING QUESTIONS, SEEKING CRITIQUE, AND CREATING DIALOGUE WITH OTHERS.

KRISTEN C. BLINNE

SO WHAT IS SEXUALITY?

We've moved from the sexological understanding of sexuality as a fixed, essential identity around a certain kind of attraction, desire, activity, or relationship, which can be categorized as normal/abnormal and explained with a universal nature/nurture theory, to something like this ...

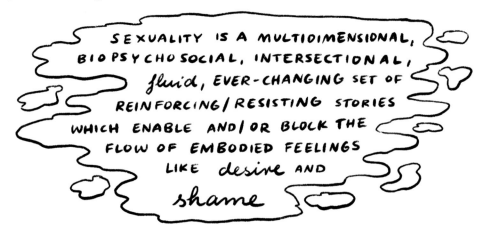

SEXUALITY IS A MULTIDIMENSIONAL, BIOPSYCHOSOCIAL, INTERSECTIONAL, fluid, EVER-CHANGING SET OF REINFORCING/RESISTING STORIES WHICH ENABLE AND/OR BLOCK THE FLOW OF EMBODIED FEELINGS LIKE desire AND shame

New stories of benign diversity, sexual fluidity, or erotic intelligence might expand erotic desires and attractions – although there's always the danger of forming new hierarchies and norms.

While we can't choose our sexuality – in the sense of forcing ourselves to conform to sexual norms – we can expand our agency and erotic potentials through the stories we engage with, the communities of support we build around us, and the erotic encounters we explore. This may enable us to experience attractions and desires outside of restrictive norms, and find activities and relationships which nourish us.

OUR VISION IS THAT RECLAIMING AND HAVING AGENCY OVER OUR BODIES WILL TRANSFER TO OTHER ASPECTS OF OUR LIVES AND INCITE US TO RECLAIM POLITICAL, ECONOMIC, AND SOCIAL AGENCY.

SEX EDUCATORS & FOUNDERS OF AFROSEXOLOGY RAFAELLA FIALLO & DALYCHIA SAAH

HETERONORMATIVITY
HOMONORMATIVITY
QUEERNESS

CHAPTER 7: CONSENT

Consent is vital to consider in relation to sexuality. This is because of the trauma caused by non-consensual sexual behaviour, and the difficulties we all have in treating others – and ourselves – consensually, within our highly non-consensual culture. While legal, and other, definitions of consent vary, they generally include people:

- **AGREEING BY CHOICE**
- **HAVING THE FREEDOM AND CAPACITY TO MAKE THAT CHOICE**

In this chapter we'll explore the conditions we would need to ensure that we, and others, are consensually agreeing to sex – and to anything else.

The current cultural conditions often mean that people who would never want to act non-consensually find themselves doing so. They also make it easier for those who want to engage in predatory sexual behaviour to do so and get away with it.

> ALMOST HALF OF WOMEN AND A QUARTER OF MEN EXPERIENCE SEXUAL ASSAULT, MOSTLY FROM PEOPLE THEY KNOW. PEOPLE OF COLOUR, TRANS PEOPLE, AND SEX WORKERS EXPERIENCE PARTICULARLY HIGH RATES.

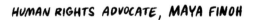

HUMAN RIGHTS ADVOCATE, MAYA FINOH

> DESPITE BEING THE BIGGEST CATEGORY OF CRIMINAL OFFENCE, SEXUAL ASSAULTS ARE RARELY REPORTED, AND THOSE THAT ARE HAVE THE LOWEST CONVICTION RATES (UNDER 6%).

YCHOLOGIST & FOUNDER OF THE CONSENT LLECTIVE, NINA BURROWES

THE CONDITIONS FOR NON-CONSENT

If we consider the conditions that make sex less likely to be consensual, we can see that the ways of understanding sex which we've covered in this book are part of the problem.

These are the conditions under which the vast majority of sex happens, and sexology, sex advice, and sex education have contributed to many of these conditions, as well as neglecting the topic of consent.

IMPLICIT CONSENT AND SEDUCTION

Let's consider the understandings of consent that circulate in wider culture, and their implications. We receive strong messages that it's sexy or romantic for people – particularly men – to continually pursue others and to behave seductively.

Ethnographer and author of *Seduction*, Rachel O'Neill points out that mainstream advice aimed at men often draws on ideas from seduction communities to advise men how to make women more compliant or less able to provide informed consent.

Sex advice often reiterates suggestions that make consent difficult or impossible. For example, it suggests that people "just do it" rather than communicating what they want, that they surprise partners with sexual scenarios, that women allow men to do or say anything they like at the point of orgasm, and that couples should have sex at a certain frequency even when they don't want it. In addition to these pressures to pursue people for sex and to perform sex rather than it being a mutual thing, there's often a "no means no" understanding of consent: Anything goes so long as the other person doesn't actively refuse it.

NO MEANS NO

"No means no" is an unrealistic expectation in a culture where people rarely use a direct "no". Feminist psychologists like Celia Kitzinger and Rachael O'Byrne found that we generally show reluctance – in both social and sexual situations – by claiming to be busy, going quiet, or changing the subject, and we do generally understand these things as meaning the same as "no".

The "no means no" approach assumes that consent is present until somebody takes it away. The emphasis is on whether the recipient refuses clearly enough, rather than whether the initiator does enough to ensure that sex is consensual.

This approach often results in mediocre sex and social encounters, as well as non-consensual ones. This is because it focuses on anything that people don't actually refuse, rather than things they actively want to do.

ENTHUSIASTIC CONSENT

A different approach which many sex educators have suggested is to flip the emphasis: the "yes means yes" model, also known as "enthusiastic consent".

ALL PARTNERS ARE RESPONSIBLE FOR ENSURING THAT THE OTHERS ARE ACTIVELY ENJOYING WHAT'S GOING DOWN BETWEEN THE TWO (OR MORE) OF YOU.

FEMINIST WRITER & EDITOR OF YES MEANS YES, JACLYN FRIEDMAN

WHAT D'YOU GUYS FANCY DOING?

I'D BE SO UP FOR GRABBING A TAKEOUT. DOES THAT WORK FOR YOU?

OH YEAH, AND MAYBE WE COULD WATCH THAT MOVIE WE ALL FANCIED?

This also requires **informed consent** because we can't say "yes" unless we know what's being proposed.

However, enthusiastic consent is difficult to achieve unless people feel able to communicate their desires openly, which few do. Also, it's tough in cultures where everyone – or certain groups – are strongly socialized to express enthusiasm for things they're not really enthusiastic about.

IT'S RFECT.

OF COURSE I'D LOVE TO COME.

STAFF ROOM

AW!

137

WANTING SEX AND CONSENTING TO SEX

There's an assumption that wanted sex is always consensual and unwanted sex is always non-consensual. Teasing this apart is important. Many asexual people, sex workers, and others do sometimes have consensual sex without wanting it. They suffer when their partners, clients, or other people insist that either it was non-consensual or that they must actually have wanted it and experienced pleasure. This denies asexual people the reality of their asexuality (see p.65).

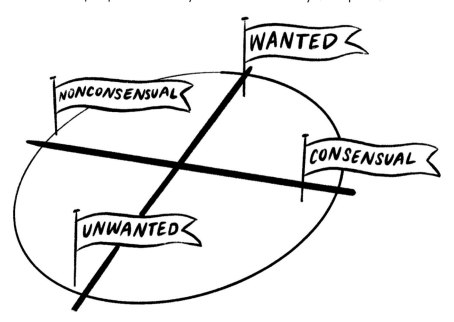

People whose consent is violated often struggle hugely if they did to some degree want sex, or experience arousal/pleasure before or during it, or if it later appears in their sexual fantasies. However, all these are common and do not legitimize the consent violation.

THIS CONFUSION BETWEEN WANTING AND CONSENTING ALSO SUPPORTS THE COMMON ASSUMPTION THAT SEX WORKERS HAVE NO AGENCY, OR DENIES THEM THE REALITY THAT THEY ARE WORKERS WHO PERFORM ENTHUSIASM AS PART OF THE EMOTIONAL LABOUR OF THEIR JOB.

SEX WORKER & WRITER, CHARLOTTE SHANE

Being clear about where we're at on this spectrum of wanting and consenting, or not, can be helpful in all aspects of life, given that people do sometimes have to do things they don't want, but they should still be able to consent.

ONGOING COMMUNICATIVE CONSENT

Some people have responded to #MeToo by creating contracts or apps whereby people can record consent prior to an encounter. This maintains consent as a one-off interaction rather than something that needs to happen throughout. People may change their mind about what they're up for, or try something and realize that it's not for them.

CONSIDER THE ACT OF UNDOING ANOTHER PERSON'S SHIRT BUTTON. NON-VERBAL RESPONSES TO THIS CLEARLY CONVEY CONSENT OR NON-CONSENT.

SEXUAL VIOLENCE RESEARCHER
MELANIE BERES

In **ongoing** or **communicative** models, sexual consent is regarded as an active process of communicating willingness. Consent is relational – between people – rather than one person initiating and the other rejecting or accepting. It involves continually choosing together between multiple options: not a sex-or-nothing binary. Ongoing checking may be verbal or non-verbal tuning in to each other's responses.

Given the research findings on the lack of communication about sex among people in long-term relationships and dating couples (see p.72), moving towards communicative models of consent would require a paradigm shift in the way most people currently engage in sex.

EXPOSING AWKWARDNESS, EMBRACING AMBIGUITY, AND ACKNOWLEDGING AMBIVALENCE ARE KEY COMPONENTS FOR SEXUAL NEGOTIATION.

CONSENT RESEARCHER
ELSIE WHITTINGTON

POWER AND CONSENT

Ensuring that everyone involved has enough freedom and capacity to choose whether to participate in something goes beyond not engaging with anyone who is drunk, high, or underage.

In the last chapter we saw how societal power structures afford some people more agency (freedom and capacity to act) than others. #MeToo highlighted the vital importance of considering the intersections of power.

Do differences in age, gender, cultural background, race, body type, disability, class, role, experience of trauma, or anything else mean we have different levels of power in a given situation? How do these affect the likely capacity of those involved to consent? How might we acknowledge and work to decrease these pressures?

CONSENT CULTURES

The consent culture movement emerged out of the BDSM community's moment of reckoning in the early 2010s (see p.81).

(see p.81)

WE REALIZED THAT NON-CONSENSUAL AND ABUSIVE DYNAMICS HAPPEN IN EVERY COMMUNITY. PEOPLE HAD COLLUDED IN KEEPING THEM HIDDEN BECAUSE OF NOT WANTING TO PLAY INTO NEGATIVE STEREOTYPES OF BDSM. I LIKENED IT TO EVERYONE WALKING AROUND A MISSING STAIR RATHER THAN ADDRESSING IT.

KINK BLOGGER & ACTIVIST CLIFF PERVOCRACY

EVERYONE ELSE THINKS HE'S GREAT ... IT MUST JUST BE ME.

I CAN'T SAY THAT HE WENT OVER MY BOUNDARIES LAST NIGHT; NO ONE WOULD BELIEVE ME.

WE CAN'T RISK THE MEDIA ATTENTION IF IT GOT OUT WHAT HE'S BEEN DOING.

IF I MENTION WHAT HAPPENED WITH HIM I'LL LOSE THE COMMUNITY.

MAYBE HE'S RIGHT AND I'M JUST NOT A GOOD ENOUGH SUB.

The consent culture movement highlights the role of power dynamics between people in limiting capacity to consent. It also acknowledges how difficult – if not impossible – it is to ensure consensual behaviour in this one area of life – sex – when our wider relationships, communities, and cultures are so often non-consensual.

CONSENT AT ALL LEVELS

Simon and Gagnon's model from the last chapter can demonstrate how our world is non-consensual at every level, making it extremely hard for us to practice consent – with ourselves and others – at the level of sexual encounters.

CONSENT IS VERY DIFFICULT UNDER THE CULTURAL HETEROSEXUAL SCRIPT. MEN ARE ASSUMED TO NATURALLY NEED SEX AND ARE SUPPOSED TO INITIATE; WOMEN AREN'T REGARDED AS ACTIVELY DESIRING, AND JUST GET TO REFUSE OR ACCEPT THE INITIATION.

FEMINIST PSYCHOLOGIST & AUTHOR OF JUST SEX ?, NICOLA GAVEY

We need to work towards more informed, ongoing consent at all levels. We need systems and structures to support us in consensual relating; we can't do it alone given the wider systems and structures are shot through with non-consent.

It's useful to think about the messages and practices we learned around consent at each level growing up, and the messages and practices around us at each level now.

I LEARNED AS A KID TO SUBMIT TO HUGS AND KISSES I DIDN'T WANT, AND IT MEANT IN LATER LIFE THAT I WENT ALONG WITH A LOT OF SEXUAL CONTACT I DIDN'T WANT EITHER.

NON-CONSENT AND INTERGENERATIONAL TRAUMA

We can see non-consensual cultures and practices as a form of intergenerational trauma passed on through the generations (see p.32). Even if the non-consent in our childhood is not sexual (which it is for many, including a third of women), most of us are forced to engage in unwanted physical touch and to put ourselves continually into dangerous situations, and are taught not to trust our feelings or bodies, to say yes when we feel no, to please others, and to feign enthusiasm.

The ancient monster in the book and film *It* who returns every generation can be seen as a metaphor for intergenerational trauma, as it reflects the way adults train children in non-consensual ways of relating to themselves and others.

These ways of relating mean that we're at far greater risk of non-consensual sex – and wider relationships – in later life, perhaps unable to even recognize it because it is so normalized and familiar.

WIDER CULTURE

The non-consensual messages we receive in our communities and relationships replicate wider non-consensual culture which, as we've seen, is predicated on treating some lives, bodies, and labour as inherently more valuable than others.

We see this link between intergenerational and historical trauma in *It*. The monster came into being around the time of settler colonialism and the genocide of indigenous Americans. Each time It reappears, it perpetrates horrors relating to the human evils that are present at the time, like racist violence in the 1930s and homophobic hate crimes in the 1980s. It holds a mirror up to the violence against ourselves, each other, other species, and the land which are the very basis of our current societies, economies, and politics.

The messages around how people should force themselves to have certain kinds of bodies, relationships, sexual activities, frequency of sex, desires, and attractions (and not others) could be regarded as a form of **social coercion**. We're told we will lose relationships, love, and approval and be shamed, stigmatized, and discriminated against if we don't conform.

COMMUNITIES AND INSTITUTIONS

In her book *Sadomasochism in Everyday Life*, sociologist Lynn Chancer writes about how school and workplace cultures push people to conform to certain notions of success, to compare themselves against others, to self-monitor and judge, to force themselves to be productive and constantly available, to accept toxic cultures and bullying, and to individualize the reasons why some do well and are rewarded and some do badly and are punished, rather than recognizing the huge role of privilege and structural injustice in this.

These non-consensual neoliberal capitalist understandings of how we should treat ourselves and others constantly creep into sex: judging our performance, being goal-focused rather than present, trying to achieve regular "success", forcing bodies to function in certain ways, aiming to "get better" at sex, etc. It's not that we're stepping over the odd missing stair (abusers who sexually harass and assault); rather that that the staircases are dangerously full of missing and broken steps because the whole culture is grounded in non-consent. Many of our communities and institutions echo the wider culture's encouragement to treat ourselves and others non-consensually. Many of our communities and institutions echo the wider culture's encouragement to treat ourselves and others non-consensually.

INTERPERSONAL RELATIONSHIPS

Sexual consent isn't possible if the wider relationship in which sex is happening is non-consensual. People often behave non-consensually in romantic - and other - relationships.

> ROMCOMS OFTEN PORTRAY BEHAVIOURS AS ROMANTIC THAT WOULD BE SEEN AS STALKING AND THEREFORE THREATENING IF ENACTED IN REAL LIFE. EXPOSURE TO THIS MEDIA CAN LEAVE PEOPLE MORE INCLINED TO BELIEVE STALKING MYTHS.

GENDER RESEARCHE
JULIA LIPPMAN

Romantic narratives also normalize attempting to cajole a partner into being what you want them to be. Cultural pressure to present relationships as perfect and keep problems private means that many people remain in damaging non-consensual dynamics. All kinds of relationships can become non-consensual - or coercive - without a common understanding of consent.

> WE HAVE TROUBLE DRAWING THE LINE WHEN IT COMES TO SEX BECAUSE FORCING PEOPLE TO DO THINGS IS PART OF OUR CULTURE. IF SOMEONE DOESN'T WANT TO GO TO A PARTY, TRY A NEW FOOD, GET UP AND DANCE, MAKE SMALL TALK AT THE LUNCH TABLE - THAT'S THEIR RIGHT. STOP THE "AWW C'MON" AND "JUST THIS ONCE" GAMES WHERE YOU PLAYFULLY FORCE SOMEONE TO PLAY ALONG.

CLIFF PERVOCRACY

SELF-CONSENT

We've generally learned to treat ourselves non-consensually too. This damages relationships, mental, and physical health.

WHEN WE'VE BEEN PREVENTED FROM LEARNING HOW TO SAY NO, OUR BODIES OFTEN END UP SAYING IT FOR US.

WE HAVE TO HAVE A CONSENSUAL RELATIONSHIP WITH OURSELVES BEFORE WE'RE CAPABLE OF CONSENTING WITH OTHERS. THAT MEANS UNDERSTANDING OUR OWN BODIES' SENSE OF "YES" AND "NO", AND OUR OWN DESIRES, NEEDS AND LIMITS.

THOR OF WHEN THE BODY SAYS NO,
R. GABOR MATÉ

SOPHIA GRAHAM

Sophia suggests learning what "yes", "no", and "maybe" feel like in our bodies by listing things we're a strong "yes" or "no" for and noticing the feelings and sensations we have when imagining or doing these things.

SPICY NOODLES IS A STRONG YES. EATING IT MAKES EVERY MUSCLE RELAX.

~DING!

CHECKING EMAILS IS A STRONG NO. MY TEETH CLENCH JUST THINKING ABOUT IT.

SELF

I DO NEED TO GET THIS TASK DONE TODAY, BUT I'M GOING TO SIT STILL FOR A MINUTE FIRST AND CHECK HOW I WANT TO GO ABOUT IT.

It's important to be gentle with ourselves because most of us have learned habits of non-self-consent over many years.

CREATING CONSENSUAL CULTURES

This exercise reveals how cultural scripts, and power disparities between people, make it hard to consent. It also introduces how we might apply open communication before an interaction, tuning in during it, and giving people multiple options.

Cultivating everyday micro-consent practices can help to shift cultures in our communities. This might include always asking somebody before touching them, and recognizing the cultural, aged, gendered, and raced entitlements that often go with touching somebody without permission.

We could also check in before starting a potentially tough topic of conversation, sharing a picture on social media, or deciding what to cook. We could make a habit of checking in before a social engagement that everyone's in a good place for it, offering alternatives, and prioritizing self-care over honouring past commitments.

PRACTICING EMBODIED CONSENT

Betty Martin's **wheel of consent®** is another helpful way into consent in practice.

IN THE 3-MINUTE GAME YOU SPEND 3 MINUTES IN PAIRS TRYING EACH QUADRANT (WITH YOUR PARTNER TAKING THE RECIPROCAL QUADRANT TO THE ONE YOU'RE IN). THE TAKER ASKS, "MAY I TOUCH YOU IN THIS WAY?" THE ACCEPTER ASKS, "WILL YOU TOUCH ME IN THIS WAY?"

BETTY MARTIN

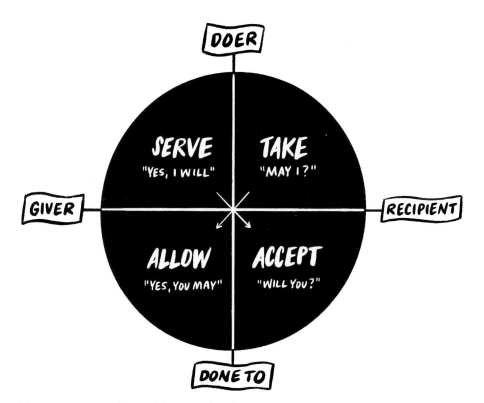

This enables us to practice asking, tuning in to our bodies when asked, and communicating and receiving agreement/refusal.

Many times in sex – and elsewhere – we give the impression that we're doing something for another person when actually it's for us (e.g. touching someone or fixing them a meal). We're in "Take" but act as if we're in "Serve". The wheel helps us to be honest, in a way that's less confusing for the other person. We can also learn which quadrants we're most comfortable and uncomfortable in, and recognize our tendencies to stray into non-consensual "shadow sides": from Taking into perpetrator; Allowing into pushover; Accepting into entitled; and Serving into martyr.

RAPE CULTURE

Rape culture normalizes, trivializes, and denies rape and blames, slut-shames, and dismisses the pain of survivors.

Rape culture means survivors often discount and hide their experiences. When our consent is violated in any way our default is often to try to figure out what we've done to invite it, to blame ourselves, to not even see that it was non-consensual, and to minimize its impact. Survivors of coercive control and other forms of gendered violence can additionally be told no abuse could have happened if no rape or sexual assault occurred.

SURVIVORS ARE PUNISHED FROM ALL SIDES. PEOPLE CUT TIES WITH THEM, SHAME THEM, AND FORCE THEM TO RELIVE THE EXPERIENCE OVER AND OVER WHILE DOUBTING AND QUESTIONING THEM ON EVERY POINT.

AUTHOR OF *THE OPPOSITE OF RAPE CULTURE IS NURTURANCE CULTURE*, NORA SAMARAN

RAPE CULTURE ENABLES US TO BELIEVE WE HAVE SOME CONTROL OVER WHETHER ASSAULT HAPPENS TO US, AND TO NOT LOOK TOO CLOSELY AT TIMES WE'VE ALL BEHAVED NON-CONSENSUALLY.

NINA BURROWE

ACCOUNTABILITY AND RESTORATIVE JUSTICE

Many have turned to restorative justice due to the non-consensual nature of the criminal legal system and its institutional racism and classism – as well as the importance of addressing all consent violations, not just those falling under legal definitions of assault.

RESTORATIVE JUSTICE PRACTITIONER SUJATHA BALIGA

THE CRIMINAL LEGAL SYSTEM DISINCENTIVIZES TRUTH-TELLING BECAUSE THOSE WHO HARM KNOW THEY'LL BE PUNISHED IF THEY ADMIT WHAT REALLY HAPPENED.

WITH ITS ROOTS IN INDIGENOUS PRACTICES, RESTORATIVE JUSTICE INVITES TRUTH-TELLING BY REPLACING PUNITIVE APPROACHES IN FAVOR OF COLLECTIVE HEALING AND SOLUTIONS. RATHER THAN ASKING, "WHAT LAW WAS BROKEN, WHO BROKE IT, AND HOW SHOULD THEY BE PUNISHED?" RESTORATIVE JUSTICE ASKS, "WHO WAS HARMED? WHAT DO THEY NEED? WHOSE OBLIGATION IS IT TO MEET THOSE NEEDS?"

Survivors generally want accountability: this involves the person who violated their consent agreeing that they are telling the truth, and affirming that they understand what they've done and won't do it again. Because sexual violence occurs and continues through shame and secrecy, restorative justice involves the family, friends, and community of all parties in separate and collective meetings. The process ends with agreed action to meet the survivor's needs and collective support to enable this.

TRANSFORMATIVE JUSTICE

Transformative justice aims to provide survivors with answers for why they were victimized, recognizing the impact, providing restitution, healing trauma, restoring peace, and enabling transformation. It often involves liaising between a survivor support team and an accountability team to work with the person responsible for the violation. Transformative justice goes beyond restorative justice in attempting to change the wider social structure as well as the personal ones of those involved.

WE NEED TO BUILD PRACTICES OF SELF-ACCOUNTABILITY — HOLDING OURSELVES RESPONSIBLE TO OUR OWN VALUES — IN ORDER TO CULTIVATE ACCOUNTABLE COMMUNITIES. DEMONIZING THOSE RESPONSIBLE FOR VIOLENCE CAN CREATE A DISCONNECT FOR SURVIVORS. EACH OF US NEEDS TO INCREASE OUR ABILITY TO HOLD THE COMPLEXITY OF SEEING SOMEONE AS A FULL HUMAN AND SEEING THE HARM THEY HAVE DONE.

ACTIVIST KIYOMI FUJIKAWA AND CONTRIBUTOR TO *THE REVOLUTION STARTS AT HOME,* SHANNON PEREZ-DARBY

TRANSFORMATIVE JUSTICE COULD BE A BETTER JUSTICE, A LOVING JUSTICE, JUSTICE THAT DOESN'T SEE VIOLENCE THROUGH THE LENS OF PERPETRATOR AND SURVIVOR ONLY BUT THAT TAKES INTO ACCOUNT THE CULPABILITY AND THE RESPONSIBILITY OF COMMUNITY.

SOCIAL WORKER & AUTHOR OF *I HOPE WE CHOOSE LOVE,* KAI CHENG THOM

CHAPTER 8: FUTURE SEX

We've seen how understandings of sexuality, pleasure, and consent are embedded within a wider capitalist, colonialist history of treating some bodies and acts as more valuable and "normal" than others. These understandings haunt the present – shaping our desires, attractions, experiences, and identities, as well as our understandings and feelings about these.

BUT WHAT'S YOUR SEXUAL ORIENTATION REALLY?

EVERYONE MUST HAVE SEX.

IT'S NOT NORMAL TO BE INTO THAT YOU KNOW.

THAT DOESN'T REALLY COUNT AS NON-CONSENT. MAYBE YOU WERE ASKING FOR IT.

SUPPORT DOG

WE LIVE IN A TIME OF GLOBAL SEX. THE SAME SEXUAL IMAGERY IS AVAILABLE ONLINE IN ANY PART OF THE WORLD AND 40% OF ALL INTERNET TRAFFIC IS SEX RELATED.

HISTORIAN & AUTHOR OF *THE PLEASURE'S ALL MINE*, **JULIE PEAKMAN**

TAKE US TO THE TIME WHEN NOBODY EVER HAS TO SAY "ME TOO" AGAIN.

In this chapter, we'll reflect on the future of sexuality. How do our present fears, such as those about the protection of children, manifest? How does sex relate to climate crisis? How might technology open up and/or close down future sexual possibilities?

OPRAH WINFREY AT THE GOLDEN GLOBE AWARDS

CHRONONORMATIVITY AND CRUEL OPTIMISM

CHRONONORMATIVITY IS THE USE OF TIME TO ORGANIZE INDIVIDUAL HUMAN BODIES TOWARD MAXIMUM PRODUCTIVITY.

QUEER THEORIST & AUTHOR OF *TIME BINDS*, ELIZABETH FREEMAN

We receive cultural messages that we should reach certain sexual checkpoints during our lives:

• INNOCENT CHILDHOOD: NO SEXUAL EXPERIENCE OR EXPRESSION

• ADOLESCENCE: APPROPRIATE EARLY SEXUAL EXPERIENCE

♥ FIRST KISS ♥

• EARLY ADULTHOOD: DATING, FINDING "THE ONE"

• MIDDLE ADULTHOOD: COMMITTING TO, AND COHABITING WITH, MONOGAMOUS PARTNER

• MIDDLE ADULTHOOD: HAVING KIDS, A PRODUCTIVE WORKING LIFE, A FULFILLING ONGOING SEX LIFE WITH PARTNER

• RETIREMENT: SEXUAL UNTIL OLD AGE WHEN IT'S NO LONGER APPROPRIATE

Very few of us pass all of these checkpoints. In this way we're all queered by life at some point: rendered non-normative. Instead of turning inwards with shame and failure, we could turn outwards and challenge these messages, recognizing that we're united in queer failure at chrononormativity. So much of what we're taught to aspire to sexually – with the promise of great pleasure, self-liberation, and happily-ever-after – actually stands in the way of us getting those things.

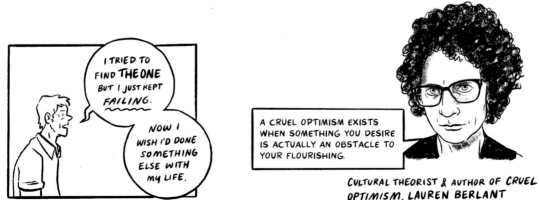

I TRIED TO FIND **THE ONE** BUT I JUST KEPT FAILING.

NOW I WISH I'D DONE SOMETHING ELSE WITH MY LIFE.

A CRUEL OPTIMISM EXISTS WHEN SOMETHING YOU DESIRE IS ACTUALLY AN OBSTACLE TO YOUR FLOURISHING.

CULTURAL THEORIST & AUTHOR OF *CRUEL OPTIMISM*, LAUREN BERLANT

SEXUALIZATION

PERHAPS THE MAIN CURRENT CONCERN ABOUT THE FUTURE OF SEX IS THE DEBATE AROUND THE SEXUALIZATION OF MEDIA AND WIDER CULTURE.

SEXUALITY SCHOLARS & AUTHORS OF THE SEXUALIZATION REPORT, FEONA ATTWOOD & CLARISSA SMITH

HYPERSEXUALIZED CULTURE IS DAMAGING US. BOYS WATCH HARDCORE ONLINE PORN. GIRLS ARE SEXUALIZED BEFORE THEY'RE OUT OF CHILDHOOD. SEX ADDICTION! TEEN PREGNANCY! SEXUAL VIOLENCE! EATING DISORDERS! STIS!

WE'VE REACHED GENDER EQUALITY AND SEXUAL LIBERATION. WE CAN BE WHAT WE WANT TO BE. FUN! CHOICE! EMPOWERMENT!

Framing this concern as an either/or debate is unhelpful. This is another manifestation of the structure/agency debate we explored in Chapter 6. Instead, we might ask how different media representations expand or contract subjects' agency.

POLARIZED DEBATES OFTEN FAIL TO TEASE APART THE DIFFERENT THINGS THAT ARE MEANT BY "SEXUALIZATION":
- SEXUAL SUGGESTIVENESS
- SEXUALLY OBJECTIFYING WOMEN
- ENCOURAGING CHILDREN TO BE ADULT/SEXUAL
- GLAMORIZING "DEVIANT" BEHAVIOUR

We need to explore how different audiences relate to and are affected by each of these four aspects of sexualization.

SOCIAL SCIENTIST & EDITOR OF PURITY AND DANGER NOW, ROBBIE DUSCHINSKY

PORN PANIC

Porn has been a central concern within the sexualization debates. Pornography is legally defined as materials "produced solely or principally for the purposes of sexual arousal". We can see the flaws in this definition and how clear categorization becomes blurred when we consider "torture porn" movies like *Saw* and *Hostel*, erotica like *Fifty Shades of Grey*, or when porn clips are circulated online for shock and humour rather than arousal, like 2 girls 1 cup.

CONTEXT MEANS SOMETHING THAT WASN'T INTENDED AS PORN CAN BECOME SO, AND SOMETHING THAT WAS PORN CEASES TO BE SO.

OBSCENITY LAWYER
MYLES JACKMAN

THE IMPACT OF PORN IS UNCLEAR. IT DEPENDS WHAT KIND WE'RE TALKING ABOUT AND HOW PEOPLE ENGAGE WITH IT. OVERALL ACCESS TO PORN DOESN'T RELATE TO LEVELS OF SEXUAL VIOLENCE. HOWEVER, ENGAGING UNCRITICALLY WITH PORN THAT NORMALIZES SEX AS BEING FOR MEN TO GET PLEASURE THROUGH DOMINANCE OR FORCE DOES RELATE TO HOLDING SEXIST ATTITUDES AND RAPE MYTHS.

THE SOCIETY FOR THE SCIENTIFIC STUDY OF SEXUALITY

CASINO ROYALE TORTURE SCENE

BEYOND PORN

The porn debate focuses on porn as the cause of sexual violence – with censorship as the solution. This shifts our attention away from the way mainstream media like romcoms, magazines, newspapers and sex advice perpetuate rape myths and normalize non-consent.

GIRLS LOVE BEING THE TIED UP HELPLESS VICTIM.

THE POSSIBILITY OF MURDER DOES BRING A CERTAIN FRISSON TO THE BEDROOM.

IF SHE WON'T PUT OUT, THINK ABOUT THIS STATISTIC: 85% OF RAPE CASES GO UNREPORTED.

WOMEN DON'T THINK THEY WANT TO HAVE SEX UNTIL THEIR GENITALS ARE FULLY STIMULATED.

IF YOU CARE FOR YOUR PARTNER, THE QUESTION SHOULDN'T BE WHETHER YOU WANT TO PROVIDE HIM WITH ORAL PLEASURE BUT RATHER HOW OFTEN!

How to Make Him Happy IN BED
A SEX GUIDE FOR WOMEN
BEST SELLER!

* ALL FROM REAL MAGAZINES & SEX ADVICE BOOKS

BLAMING PORN ALSO DISTRACTS FROM THE ROLE OF CULTURAL BIAS AND STRUCTURAL INEQUALITY IN CRIME AND IN THE CRIMINAL JUSTICE SYSTEM. FOR EXAMPLE, WE KNOW THAT RAPE MYTHS AND SYSTEMIC RACISM HAVE A HUGE IMPACT ON JUROR DECISIONS.

NINA BURROWES

We could consider how to make a more diverse range of sexual media available, and teach people how to critically engage with all the media they access, instead of panicking at each new wave of media and technology.

YOUNG PEOPLE AND SEX

Childhood has been a key focus of the sexualization panic. Conflicting cultural messages around sex and childhood make this challenging terrain, for example: youth is highly eroticized in wider culture. However, attraction to children and young people is heavily stigmatized, making it hard for those who do experience such desires to navigate them consensually.

CHILDREN AND YOUNG PEOPLE EXPERIENCE SEXUAL FEELINGS, OFTEN FROM A YOUNG AGE, AND PARTICULARLY DURING PUBERTY. HOWEVER, THEY ARE EXPECTED TO BE INNOCENT AND ASEXUAL, AND SHAMED AND PUNISHED FOR NOT BEING SO – ESPECIALLY IF THEY ARE QUEER, WORKING-CLASS, AND/OR OF COLOUR.

GENDER SCHOLAR & AUTHOR OF *BECOMING SEXUAL*, R. DANIELLE EGAN

Anxieties around sex and young people focus on stranger predators online and offline, when by far the greatest risk is from known people at school and home. There's little information to help children identify and speak about sexual behaviour from peers and/or adults in their lives. The focus on sex as the key danger to young people also means that the traumatizing impact of other forms of bullying and abuse is frequently minimized, denied, or presented as a normal part of childhood.

CHILDHOOD CONCERNS

CHILDHOOD IS WHEN WE LEARN THE MESSAGES ABOUT RELATIONSHIPS, BODIES, AND FEELINGS THAT OFTEN LAST OUR LIFETIME. BUT THERE ARE BIG ANXIETIES FROM PARENTS, TEACHERS, AND DOCTORS ABOUT TALKING OPENLY ABOUT SEX WITH YOUNG PEOPLE, MEANING FEW GET ANYWHERE NEAR THE EDUCATION THEY NEED.

MEDIA SCHOLAR **ANNE-FRANCES WATSON**

It's telling that sexualization concerns focus on representations that lead people away from normativity and not those that lead people towards it. Anxieties focus on the sexualizing of toys and clothes (taking children away from the ideal of innocence) and teaching young people about sexual diversity (opening up the possibility of a non-heteronormative life). There's much less concern about everyday sexual harassment and homophobic bullying that are common features of kids' lives.

Young people are rarely taught about pleasure or desire, due to concerns this would make STIS or teen pregnancy more likely. They're often explicitly or implicitly taught that abstinence is the ideal. There's no evidence that accurate sex education makes children more likely to engage in it, but education on diversity, pleasure, and consent does make it more likely that they'll protect themselves and communicate openly with partners if they are sexual.

KIDS ONLINE

Considering childhood sexuality in relation to pleasure, not just danger, can enable us to see what technological possibilities like sexting, online porn, or selfies might open up – as well as close down.

WE FOUND THAT SEXTING WAS OFTEN COERCIVE, WITH GIRLS PARTICULARLY PEER-PRESSURED INTO IT.

FEMINIST SOCIOLOGIST
LAURA HARVEY

WHEN CONSENSUAL THOUGH, IT'S LINKED TO SEXUAL SATISFACTION AND SAFER SEX. IT CAN MEAN YOUNG PEOPLE ENGAGE IN SEXUAL PRACTICES PRIOR TO INVOLVING THEIR BODIES, HELPING THEM TO LEARN ABOUT AND COMMUNICATE THEIR DESIRES.

SEX RESEARCHER & HOST OF "SEX ED SCHOOL", *EVA BLOOM*

Media scholar Alan McKee found that porn can feature within healthy sexual development by helping young people learn about what they enjoy, communicate with partners, and understand that sex should be joyful rather than coercive. But porn doesn't foster the skills necessary for safer, consensual sex, so sex education is required to plug those gaps.

THIS IS GIVING ME LOTS OF IDEAS

I DON'T KNOW HOW TO EXPERIENCE THIS SAFELY.

 EROTICA

WE NEED TO GET YOUNG PEOPLE ENGAGING CRITICALLY WITH ALL TYPES OF MEDIA, ENABLING EXPLORATION OF SEXUALITY AND SEXUAL DESIRE OUTSIDE OF THE LIMITS OF EUROCENTRIC BEAUTY STANDARDS AND HETERONORMATIVITY.

SEX EDUCATOR & AUTHOR OF *BEHIND CLOSED DOORS, NATALIE FIENES*

CHILDREN ARE THE FUTURE

THE CURRENT SYSTEM MAKES IT VERY DIFFICULT TO TEACH CHILDREN ABOUT CONSENT, WHEN THEY ARE TREATED NON-CONSENSUALLY, REGARDED AS PROPERTY OF ADULTS, AND DENIED AGENCY THROUGHOUT CHILDHOOD.

JUSTIN HANCOCK

EXCLUDING CHILDREN FROM KNOWLEDGE ABOUT SEXUALITY IMPACTS THEIR HEALTH, WELLBEING, AGENCY AND DEVELOPMENT.

SOCIOLOGIST & AUTHOR OF *INNOCENCE, KNOWLEDGE, AND THE CONSTRUCTION OF CHILDHOOD*, KERRY ROBINSON

Sex advice and education for kids centres on protection from danger, whereas for adults it centres on demonstrating pleasure, with very little mention of consent or potential risks. Both are problematic and potentially put people at risk of exploitation and abuse.

CHILDREN ARE TOO YOUNG TO KNOW WHAT THEY WANT...

...OR NEED!

I'M FORCED TO EAT FOODS I HATE.

MY GRAND-PARENTS KISS ME WHEN I DON'T WANT THEM TO, BUT WHEN A CLASSMATE AND I KISSED, EVERYONE GOT REALLY ANGRY.

The question of children's agency and rights has been given greater focus thanks to the school climate strikes and the environmental activist Greta Thunberg, who has raised the question of intergenerational justice.

THE EYES OF ALL FUTURE GENERATIONS ARE UPON YOU. IF YOU CHOOSE TO FAIL US, WE WILL NEVER FORGIVE YOU.

GRETA THUNBERG

SEXECOLOGY AND ECOSEXUALITY

ECOSEXUALITY EXPANDS OUR OPPORTUNITIES FOR PLEASURE. AS WELL AS THE IDEA OF MOTHER EARTH, WHERE THE EARTH COMFORTS YOU, EARTH IS YOUR LOVER – ON YOUR LEVEL – PUTTING THE RESPONSIBILITY ON YOU TO UPHOLD YOUR SIDE OF THE RELATIONSHIP. IT'S REVOLUTIONARY.

BETH STEPHENS & ANNIE SPRINKLE

Artist Beth Stephens and feminist sex educator Annie Sprinkle, authors of *Assuming the Ecosexual Position*, are developing our understanding of "sexecology" and "ecosexuality", forms of sexuality that make a connection between the environment, activism, and sex.

We've seen how our capitalist, colonialist systems value certain lives and bodies over others – and how this affects non-consensual sex. We can also link this to how humans have been valued over other species and the planet. Exploring our sexuality in relation to nature offers the potential for a greater understanding of our interdependence, which can engage us politically and spiritually, as well as erotically.

… WE SHAMELESSLY HUG TREES, MASSAGE THE EARTH WITH OUR FEET, AND TALK EROTICALLY TO PLANTS. WE ARE SKINNY DIPPERS, SUN WORSHIPPERS, AND STARGAZERS. WE CARESS ROCKS, ARE PLEASURED BY WATERFALLS, AND ADMIRE THE EARTH'S CURVES. WE MAKE LOVE WITH THE EARTH THROUGH OUR SENSES. WE CELEBRATE OUR E-SPOTS. WE ARE VERY DIRTY.

THE ECOSEXUAL MANIFESTO

PLEASURE ACTIVISM

Sex, and technologies enabling sexual experiences, can be forces for distancing us from ourselves, others, and the world, or for connecting us, as has been explored in popular movies over the years.

BRIDE OF FRANKENSTEIN

BARBARELLA

I LIVE IN A HIGHLY EXCITED STATE OF OVERSTIMULATION.

VIDEODROME

In *Emergent Strategy*, pleasure activist Adrienne Maree Brown writes about tapping into our desires to organize against oppression.

BLACK PEOPLE HAVE BEEN TOLD, "YOU'RE 3/5 OF A PERSON." IF YOU DON'T FEEL FULLY HUMAN, THEN HOW CAN YOU BELIEVE YOU HAVE ACCESS? WHEN INDIGENOUS PEOPLE ARE LIVING WITH THE EFFECTS OF GENOCIDE, HOW ARE THEY SUPPOSED TO FIND PLEASURE? IT'S ABOUT RECLAIMING OUR BIRTHRIGHT.

ADRIENNE MAREE BROWN

WE NEED A GLOBAL, RADICAL, UNAPOLOGETIC SELF-LOVE WHICH TRANSLATES TO RADICAL HUMAN LOVE AND ACTION IN SERVICE TOWARD A MORE JUST, EQUITABLE AND COMPASSIONATE WORLD.

AUTHOR & FOUNDER OF THE BODY IS NOT AN APOLOGY MOVEMENT, SONYA RENEE TAYLOR

Experiencing our sexuality fully, and understanding how aspects of it are marginalized or pathologized, can connect us with all oppression and motivate us to engage politically.

Joy through erotic experience can enable us to see what's possible when we're free and treated consensually; to demand that from all aspects of our lives. Self-pleasure and pleasure with others can enable the gruelling work of tackling oppression and climate crisis.

HAVING OR BEING SEX

How do we move towards a future where erotic engagements enable better lives for all? We could shift from a "having" to "being" approach to sex – and to everything else.

> HAVING IS WHEN WE'RE TRYING TO GET THINGS FOR OURSELVES, AND BEING IS WHEN WE'RE PRESENT TO WHAT IS.

PHILOSOPHER **ERICH FROMM**

> THIS RELATES TO MY IDEA OF LOVE AS SOMETHING WE DO WITH OTHER PEOPLE WHEN WE TREAT OURSELVES AND THEM AS EQUALLY VALUABLE, AND ALL OF US AS INTERCONNECTED.

FEMINIST & AUTHOR OF ALL ABOUT LOVE, bell hooks

Capitalism is in "having" mode, promising individuals unlimited happiness, material abundance, and domination of nature if they follow normative rules. In sex this results in a goal-focused approach where we try to get what we (think we should) want. More widely it results in people asserting their agency above that of partners and others, including children and the planet.

We need to move – individually and culturally – towards "being" mode: recognizing that no bodies or acts are inherently more valuable or "normal" than others, and that it's about mutuality rather than getting something from someone, and being present rather than reaching a goal.

CHAPTER 9 : RETHINKING SEX

Throughout this book we've seen how current Western understandings about sex and sexuality limit erotic experience, stigmatize people, and underpin discriminatory and non-consensual practices.

These understandings have been passed on through historical and intergenerational trauma and passed around through colonialism and globalization. They're inextricably linked to white supremacy, patriarchal oppression, capitalism, ableism, and other forms of marginalization where certain lives, bodies and relations are valued far more highly than others. So what do we need to do?

UNLEARNING EVERYTHING WE KNOW ABOUT SEX

What do we need to unlearn about sex, and what might we put in its place? Let's return to two key thinkers who've informed this book: Gayle Rubin and Audre Lorde.

WE'VE LEARNED ABOUT CULTURAL BINARIES THAT LIMIT WHAT COUNTS AS GOOD/NORMAL AND BAD/ABNORMAL SEX. WE NEED TO MOVE TOWARDS A RECOGNITION OF BENIGN SEXUAL DIVERSITY AND A FOCUS ON PLEASURE AND CONSENT.

GAYLE RUBIN

WE'VE LEARNED TO NARROW OUR EROTIC IMAGINATION TO CERTAIN FORMS OF SEX. WE NEED TO TUNE INTO THE FULL POTENTIAL OF THE EROTIC TO CHALLENGE INNER AND OUTER OPPRESSION AND TO ACHIEVE PERSONAL AND POLITICAL TRANSFORMATION, AND WE NEED COMMUNITIES WITHIN WHICH TO DO THIS.

AUDRE LORDE

Both authors emphasize learning from the margins. Instead of trying to classify and explain marginal sexualities, as sexology has tended to do, what if we recognized the margins as the zone in which the most innovative, critical, and creative thinking around sex often occurs? Instead of viewing the marginalized parts of our sexualities as something to hide, we might embrace them as something to celebrate and cultivate, acknowledging the ways in which we're all marginal and queered by life (see pp. 112 and 153).

ENSURING LIVABLE LIVES

Philosopher Judith Butler points out that current cultural norms often prevent marginalized people from having "livable lives". Often people have tried to ensure more livable lives by aiming for acceptance within normativity. However, this retains the harmful normative system. How can we imagine better futures for ourselves without perpetuating narrow sexual norms?

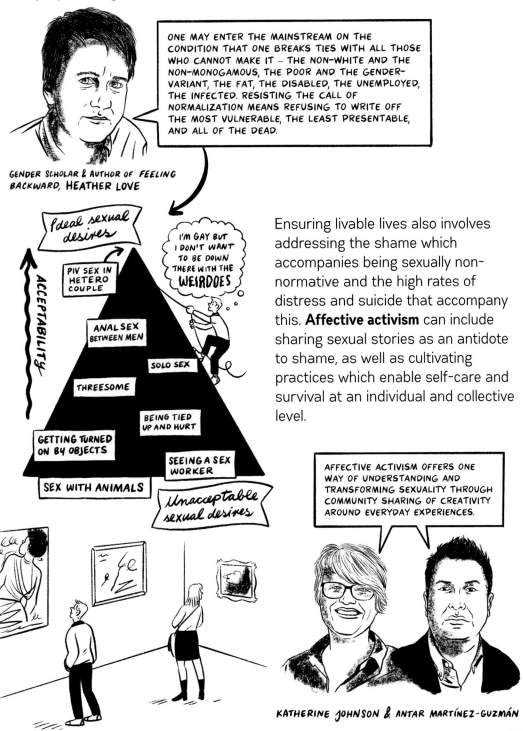

ONE MAY ENTER THE MAINSTREAM ON THE CONDITION THAT ONE BREAKS TIES WITH ALL THOSE WHO CANNOT MAKE IT – THE NON-WHITE AND THE NON-MONOGAMOUS, THE POOR AND THE GENDER-VARIANT, THE FAT, THE DISABLED, THE UNEMPLOYED, THE INFECTED. RESISTING THE CALL OF NORMALIZATION MEANS REFUSING TO WRITE OFF THE MOST VULNERABLE, THE LEAST PRESENTABLE, AND ALL OF THE DEAD.

GENDER SCHOLAR & AUTHOR OF *FEELING BACKWARD*, HEATHER LOVE

Ideal sexual desires

ACCEPTABILITY

PIV SEX IN HETERO COUPLE

I'M GAY BUT I DON'T WANT TO BE DOWN THERE WITH THE WEIRDOES

ANAL SEX BETWEEN MEN

SOLO SEX

THREESOME

BEING TIED UP AND HURT

GETTING TURNED ON BY OBJECTS

SEEING A SEX WORKER

SEX WITH ANIMALS

Unacceptable sexual desires

Ensuring livable lives also involves addressing the shame which accompanies being sexually non-normative and the high rates of distress and suicide that accompany this. **Affective activism** can include sharing sexual stories as an antidote to shame, as well as cultivating practices which enable self-care and survival at an individual and collective level.

AFFECTIVE ACTIVISM OFFERS ONE WAY OF UNDERSTANDING AND TRANSFORMING SEXUALITY THROUGH COMMUNITY SHARING OF CREATIVITY AROUND EVERYDAY EXPERIENCES.

KATHERINE JOHNSON & ANTAR MARTÍNEZ-GUZMÁN

CHALLENGING INNER AND OUTER OPPRESSION

Unlearning the understandings of sex that hurt us all requires a wider ongoing project of queering and decolonizing our minds and bodies, and dismantling the capitalist and patriarchal systems which uphold these understandings. With such a huge project, how can we handle the inevitable grief, shame, and fear that arise around our own experiences of oppression? How can we confront areas where we're implicated in the oppression of others, without defending or collapsing under the idea of ourselves as monstrous?

ANTI-OPPRESSION PEDAGOGY OFFERS EMBODIED AND RELATIONAL PRACTICES FOR INTERRUPTING OPPRESSION AT ITS ROOT IN OUR BODIES, HEARTS AND MINDS.

Teaching to Transgress — bell hooks

pedagogy of the oppressed — PAULO FREIRE

GENDER & WOMEN'S STUDIES PROFESSOR, BETH BERILA

I'M IN A GROUP WHERE WE SHARE OUR EXPERIENCES AND WORK ON THE AREAS WE STRUGGLE WITH TOGETHER.

I'VE LEARNED HOW TRAUMA WORKS IN THE BODY, SO I'M BETTER ABLE TO NOTICE WHEN I'M GETTING DEFENSIVE IN A CONVERSATION AND TAKE TIME OUT.

I'M WORKING ON SELF-COMPASSION SO THAT I DON'T FALL INTO SHAME SO MUCH.

I'M LEARNING HOW TO STAY WITH UNCOMFORTABLE FEELINGS AND REALLY LISTEN TO OTHERS ABOUT THE IMPACT SYSTEMIC PRIVILEGE HAS ON THEM.

OPENING UP OUR SEXUAL AGENCY

Our freedom is constrained by the cultural understandings available to us and wider social structures. How can we open up sexual agency?

THE CO-EVOLUTION OF IDENTITIES AND FEELINGS, AND WORDS TO DESCRIBE THEM, PROVIDE SCRIPTS FOR WHAT WE CAN BE.

AUTHOR OF *TRANS BRITAIN*, CHRISTINE BURNS

ACE TERMS LIKE "SQUISH" AND "QUEERPLATONIC" HELP ME UNDERSTAND MYSELF.

QTIPOC BURLESQUE WAS POLITICALLY AND PERSONALLY TRANSFORMATIVE FOR ME.

WHITE SUPREMACY IS DESIGNED TO ALIENATE, CONTROL, AND DESTROY US. RECLAIMING OUR BLACK BODIES AND SEXUALITY IS IN DIRECT OPPOSITION TO THIS SYSTEM AND AN ACT OF RESISTANCE.

AFROSEXOLOGY

QUEER SPACES AND PRACTICES CAN CHANGE SOCIETY FOR THE BETTER BY DISRUPTING GENDER STEREOTYPES, BODY NORMATIVITY, AND SEXUAL SCRIPTS, FINDING NEW WAYS TO EXPERIENCE BODIES, PLEASURES, AND POWER.

AUTHOR OF *QUEER SEX*, JUNO ROCHE

SELF-PLEASURE GROUP SHOWED ME WHAT MY SEXUALITY COULD BE, UNRELATED TO PARTNER EXPECTATIONS.

However, new systems can close down agency as well as opening it up, requiring critical engagement with new norms and emergent hierarchies within communities.

EMBRACING SEXUAL DIVERSITY

If one of the biggest restrictions around sexuality is the normal/abnormal distinction, what does embracing benign sexual diversity look like?

CREATING THE CONDITIONS FOR CONSENSUAL SEX AND RELATIONSHIPS

What conditions make consent more likely?

Informed consent is the aim

Ongoing and relational consent

Power awareness and accountability

CULTIVATING CONSENT CULTURES

Given our non-consensual wider culture, how can we cultivate micro-cultures of consent?

- Support each other to learn how our bodies feel when we're in self-consent and when we're overriding it, so we can tune into our desires and limits.
- Practice self-care and consent with friends/colleagues.
- Model talking openly about times we haven't been consensual in minor ways and being accountable.
- Form supportive groups for when consent violations happen.

The lines can be unclear between sex and play, leisure, art, and spirituality. People are nervous about this due to risks of exploitation, harassment, and abuse if non-sexual situations stray into sexual. Instead of distinguishing sex from not-sex, we could focus on distinguishing consent from non-consent across all situations. Consensual sex is hard – if not impossible – if the rest of our lives are non-consensual, and the rest of our lives should be consensual too.

EXPANDING OUR EROTIC IMAGINATIONS

If we can embrace benign sexual diversity and consent, we can begin to expand our erotic imaginations to include everything we might find pleasurable alone and/or with others, in nurturing and/or erotic ways.

We might try remembering in detail a time when a sexual or sensual activity made us feel alive and a time when it didn't (Chapter 3). What key features distinguished these times?

We might create yes/no/maybe lists (p.72), explore what different practices mean to us (p.69), tune into our sexual fantasies (p.126), and explore various contexts for connection (Chapter 5). This can help us to communicate our desires with each other, finding areas of overlap, and respecting boundaries and limits.

If we fully appreciate that solo sex and fantasy are legitimate, and that all forms of erotic activity and connection are equally valid, it can be easier to stay in consent, enjoy some activities or desires alone, and find ways to roleplay fantasies that wouldn't be acceptable to really act upon. We can also establish relationships in which nobody is ever pressured to do something they're not into.

APPROACHING SEX AS A PERSONAL/POLITICAL PRACTICE

The capacities we develop from rethinking sex can help towards personal and political transformation.

I'M TRYING TO BE A FORCE FOR GENTLY CHALLENGING NORMATIVE SCRIPTS AND IDEAS OF "SUCCESS" WHEREVER I SEE THEM. WITHIN MY COMMUNITY IT'S BEEN SO HELPFUL TO SHIFT FROM ALWAYS STRIVING TO REACH A GOAL, TO ENSURING THAT THE PROCESS IS WORKING FOR EVERYONE.

I'VE REALIZED THAT BEING PRESENT WITH MYSELF AND OTHER PEOPLE IS VITAL FOR GOOD SEX. PRACTICING THAT IN SEX HAS HELPED ME TO BE MORE PRESENT TO THE REST OF MY LIFE TOO, LIKE REALLY EXPERIENCING WHAT I'M GOING THROUGH AND LISTENING DEEPLY TO OTHER PEOPLE.

ENGAGING WITH MY COMMUNITY HAS HELPED ME TO UNDERSTAND HOW OPPRESSION AND SHAME WORK. I'M NOW TRYING TO LEARN ABOUT OPPRESSIONS BEYOND MY PERSONAL EXPERIENCE, AND TO EDUCATE OTHERS ABOUT HOW NO LIVES, BODIES, OR DESIRES ARE INTRINSICALLY MORE OR LESS VALUABLE THAN OTHERS.

WHAT I'VE LEARNED ABOUT MY DESIRES AND LIMITS IN ORDER TO ENSURE CONSENSUAL SEX HAS HELPED ME TO NOTICE AND EXPRESS MY NEEDS AND BOUNDARIES IN OTHER AREAS OF LIFE, AND TO ENCOURAGE OTHERS TO DO SO AS WELL.

FURTHER RESOURCES

We drew on some key resources to write this book:

- McCann, C. (2018). *All You Need to Know... Sexuality*. London: Connel Publishing.
- Mottier, V. (2008). *Sexuality: A Very Short Introduction*. Oxford: Oxford University Press.
- Barker, M-J. (2018). *The Psychology of Sex*. London: Routledge and Psychology Press.
- Weeks, J. (2003). *Sexuality*. London: Routledge.
- Smith, C., Atwood, F., Egan, R. D. & McNair, B. (Eds.) (2017). *Routledge Companion to Media, Sex and Sexuality*. London: Routledge.
- Johnson, K. (2015). *Sexuality: A Psychosocial Manifesto*. Cambridge: Polity Press.
- Jackson, S. & Scott, S. (2010). *Theorizing Sexuality*. Maidenhead: Open University Press.
- Lister, K. (2019). *A Curious History of Sex*. London: Unbound.
- Peakman, J. (2013). *The Pleasure's All Mine*. London: Reaktion Books.
- Fucked zine: fuckedzine.tumblr.com
- Chen, C. I., Dulani, J., & Piepzna-Samarasinha, L. L. (Eds.). (2011). *The revolution starts at home*. Brooklyn, NY: South End Press.
- Transform harm: transformharm.org
- Building accountable communities: survivedandpunished.org
- The Sexualization Report: thesexualizationreport.wordpress.com
- Berila, B. (2016). *Integrating Mindfulness into Anti-Oppression Pedagogy*. London: Routledge

We've mentioned as many writings of sexuality theorists and activists as possible throughout the book so you can search them out; two classic essays we love the most are:

Lorde, A. (1984). The uses of the erotic: The erotic as power. In A. Lorde (2012). *Sister outsider: Essays and speeches*. Berkeley, CA: Crossing Press.

Rubin, G. (1984). Thinking sex: Notes for a radical theory of the politics of sexuality. In G. Rubin (2012). *Deviations: A Gayle Rubin Reader*. Durham, NC: Duke University Press.

The following books and websites are great if you want to think more about sex and sexuality in your everyday life.

Barker, M-J. & Hancock, J. (2017). *Enjoy sex (How, when and if you want to)*. London: Icon Books.

Barker, M-J. & Iantaffi, A. (2021). *How to Understand Your Sexuality*. London: JKP.

Hancock, J. (2021). *Can we talk about consent?* London: Frances Lincoln.

Moen, E. (2016). *Oh joy sex toy*. Portland, OR: Oni Press.

Perry, F. (2019). *How to have feminist sex*. London: Penguin.

Morin, J. (1995). *The erotic mind*. London: Headline.

Also, check out the zines, podcasts, and posts about sex and sexuality on Meg-John's website rewriting-the-rules.com.

Finally, several Icon books expand upon material covered in this book. Check out our Graphic Guides to *Queer*, *Gender*, *Foucault*, *Feminism*, *Critical Theory*, and *Cultural Studies*.

ACKNOWLEDGEMENTS

Meg-John would like to thank Kiera Jamison, Jules Scheele, H Howitt, Justin Hancock, Eleanor Janega, Alex Iantaffi, Nina Burrowes and Cynthia Ellis for all their help and support during the writing of this book.

Jules would like to thank Adrian May for all the encouragement, support, patience, kindness, and tea. I couldn't have done this year without you.

BIOGRAPHIES

Meg-John Barker is the author of many popular books on sex, gender, and relationships, including *Queer: A Graphic History* and *Gender: A Graphic Guide* (with Jules Scheele), *How To Understand Your Gender* and *Life Isn't Binary* (with Alex Iantaffi), *Enjoy Sex (How, When, and IF You Want To)* (with Justin Hancock), *Rewriting the Rules*, and *The Psychology of Sex*. They've also written numerous books, articles, chapters, and reports for scholars and counsellors, drawing on their own research and therapeutic practice in these areas. They blog and podcast about these topics on rewriting-the-rules.com and megjohnandjustin.com and they're available for talks, workshops, and writing mentorship.
Twitter: @megjohnbarker.

Jules Scheele is a non-binary illustrator who specialises in graphic storytelling and illustrations that help translate and bring a human touch to difficult concepts. Their art and comics focus strongly on mental health, queerness, activism and community. Selected past clients include The Scottish Books Trust, The Guardian, Image Comics, Dark Horse Books, Routledge, International Progressive Review, Edinburgh International Television Festival, Kerrang!, BBC, Open University, Close Up Research, NHS, and Scottish Political Archive. From 2014-18 Jules ran One Beat Zines, a feminist zine collective and distro. They also co-organise Ghost Comics Festival in Glasgow, which showcases independent and alternative comics artists.
Twitter: @julesscheele.
Instagram: @julesscheeleillustration.